Untie Every kNOT

Untie Every kNOT

Discover What kNOTS Are Causing You to Miss Out, Chicken Out or Be Counted Out!

TAMMY TILLER-HEWITT

IGNITE PRESS
Fresno, CA

Copyright © 2020, Tammy Tiller-Hewitt

All rights reserved. No part of this book may be used or reproduced by any means, graphic, electronic, or mechanical (including any information storage retrieval system) without the express written permission from the author, except in the case of brief quotations for use in articles and reviews wherein appropriate attribution of the source is made.

Published in the United States by Ignite Press.
ignitepress.us

ISBN: 978-1-950710-72-0 (Amazon Print)
ISBN: 978-1-950710-73-7 (IngramSpark) PAPERBACK
ISBN: 978-1-950710-74-4 (IngramSpark) HARDCOVER
ISBN: 978-1-950710-75-1 (Smashwords)

For bulk purchase and for booking, contact:

Tammy Tiller-Hewitt
tth@tillerhewitt.com
UntieEverykNOT.com

Because of the dynamic nature of the Internet, web addresses or links contained in this book may have been changed since publication and may no longer be valid. The content of this book and all expressed opinions are those of the author and do not reflect the publisher or the publishing team. The author is solely responsible for all content included herein.

Library of Congress Control Number: 2020916547

Cover design by Nenad Cvetkovski
Edited by Samantha Maxwell
Interior design by Evolve Layout Services

"Where God guides He provides" has become my battle cry because every single time I've given my burdens to Him and have trusted Him, He has set me free. Who wouldn't stand firmly on His promise that *No eye has seen, no ear has heard, no mind can conceive the wonderful things He has in store for those who love Him?* This book is just one example of how God continues fulfilling His promises to me. This book was a kNOT that would never have been untied without Him.

I pray that reading this book will do the same for you!

I dedicate this book to the One who makes the sun rise for you and me every single morning.

Acknowledgements

To my husband, Jeff, who makes me better and treats me like his queen every single day.

To my children, Tommy & Taylor, for giving my life meaning and giving me a reason to model the way. You are two humans who continue to make me the proudest mom on planet earth.

To my parents, Gloria & Les, who stayed together through thick and thin, who made growing up fun and memorable, for modeling the way, and never tolerating your children tying kNOTs around any dream.

To my editorial board, Cathy Fyock, Lauren Dauksch, Mary Reilly, Kimberly Tiller, and Mom - your honest feedback and support was invaluable.

To my sisters, Andrea & Kathy, for always being my biggest fans, encouraging me every step of the way.

To GOD: For giving me life, gifts, and talents, but most of all for putting your Son in my place so my future is secure in YOU.

Preface

This book is about kNOTS: little k, big NOTS. It's about the kNOTs we tie around ourselves, around our dreams, our purpose, and even around our God-given destinies. It's about the kNOTs we subscribe to or blame others for binding. We can get so tangled up in our own kNOTS that it's nearly impossible to recognize their paralyzing, life-limiting, dream-smashing grip.

Knots, unlike *kNOTS*, can serve an important purpose. The problem is their purpose becomes so blurred that instead of serving as a temporary safety handle, they become a permanent death-gripping stronghold.

I wrote this book so together we can learn to identify and forever untie the Gordian-sized kNOTS holding us back. This book is for anyone who has allowed a kNOT to cause them to miss out, chicken out, or be counted out.

Think of this book as a conversation between two friends. We may laugh, cry, and perhaps debate—but in the end, we're friends.

Minds are like parachutes, they work best when they are open.

TABLE OF CONTENTS

INTRODUCTION 1

CHAPTER 1: The Thing About kNOTS 3

CHAPTER 2: Clarity Over Complication 17

CHAPTER 3: Head or Heart Condition 27

CHAPTER 4: Knowing the End of the Story 33

CHAPTER 5: Regret-Proof 49

CHAPTER 6: Size Matters: Be Embarrassed 55

CHAPTER 7: Rejection-Proof Yourself 61

CHAPTER 8: You Were Made for More 67

CHAPTER 9: Excuses, Excuses: Burn Your Bucket 77

CHAPTER 10: You Go First, but Don't Be Weird 85

CHAPTER 11: Show Me Your Friends 93

CHAPTER 12: Let *Your* Life Shine 101

- CHAPTER 13: NOW Is Your Time 109
- CHAPTER 14: Untie Your kNOTS to Finish Grand 121
- CONCLUSION 129
- ENDNOTES 135
- ABOUT THE AUTHOR 137

INTRODUCTION

Abraham Lincoln once said, when you reach the end of your rope, tie a knot and hang on. The kNOTS I'm talking about in this book are much different—almost opposite—because *they're not* something you want to hang on to.

This book is about kNOTS—little k, big NOTS. It's about the kNOTS we tie around ourselves, around our dreams, our purpose, and even around our God-given destinies. It's about the kNOTS we subscribe to or blame others for binding. We can get so tangled up in our own kNOTS that it's nearly impossible to recognize their paralyzing, life-limiting, dream-smashing grip.

 Breakthroughs happen when your kNOTS intersect the end of your rope.

CHAPTER 1

THE THING ABOUT KNOTS

Untying kNOTS unlocks potential.

Knots, unlike *kNOTS*, can serve an important purpose. The problem is their purpose becomes so blurred that instead of serving as a temporary safety handle, they become a permanent death-gripping stronghold.

GORDIAN KNOTS & ALEXANDER THE GREAT

The term "Gordian knot," is often used in reference to an extremely difficult or involved problem. Its origin can be traced back to the life of Alexander the Great. As the story goes, in 333 B.C., Alexander marched his army into the capital of Gordium (modern-day Turkey). Upon arriving in the city, he encountered an ancient wagon tied with what one Roman historian later described as "several knots, all so tightly entangled that it was impossible to see how they were fastened."

Tradition held the wagon had once belonged to Gordius, the father of the King. A prophet declared that any man who could unravel its elaborate knots was destined to become ruler of Asia.

According to history, the impulsive Alexander was instantly obsessed with untying the Gordian knot. After wrestling with it for a while with no success, he stepped back and declared, "It makes no difference how they are loosed." He then drew his sword and sliced the knot in half with a single stroke.

Alexander was immediately hailed as having outsmarted the ancient puzzle. True to the prophecy, he went on to conquer Egypt and large portions of Asia.

Thanks to the popularity of the legend, the phrase "Gordian knot" has become known as an intricate or problematic obstacle. Likewise, the saying "cutting the Gordian knot" is now commonly used to describe a creative or decisive solution to a seemingly insurmountable problem.

Funny recent story: I read about a residential door-lock company named The Gordian Knot. Their tagline is *"They'll never undo this sucker."* I wonder how many of their customers locked themselves out of their own houses. The morale of the story: We don't want any Gordian kNOTs in our lives!

I wrote this book so together we can learn to identify and forever untie the Gordian-sized kNOTS holding us back. This book is for anyone who has allowed a kNOT to cause them to miss out, chicken out, or be held back from living the unbelievable life and destiny God designed just for you.

YOUR kNOTS: SMALL OR GORDIAN-SIZED?

I want to talk to you about the kNOT or kNOTS that prevent growth and are likely self-imposed lies, something like you're kNOT good enough, you're kNOT smart enough, you're kNOT whatever enough! Let's figure out a way to uncover and better understand the what, how, and why of kNOTS holding us back.

THE WHAT IF

What if? Now that's a short but loaded question. Playing the "WHAT IF" game is one of my favorite games. By design, it's exciting, should automatically remove inhibitions, drown out my negativity, and force me to realize most of my impossibilities are self-imposed and are in fact very possible. Want to play?

 What if... "NOT" was no longer a word in your vocabulary?

Let's start with this: What if... "NOT" was no longer a word in your vocabulary? What if... starting this very minute—regardless of your age, race, gender, or shoe size—you could no longer use any form of the word NOT as it relates to your abilities, your dreams, or your potential? Come on. Just give it some thought! What if...? We're basically starting with what we want—not if or how we get there. That is exactly how we start uncovering our own kNOTS. Pause and jot down a list of your dreams, desires, and goals without any kNOTS. I shared one of mine in each category. Don't stop at just one, but at least write in one!

DREAMS	DESIRES	GOALS
Example: Lead millions to discover their WHY (their purpose).	**Example:** Be someone people (especially my family) want and love being around.	**Example:** Speak to national and international audiences about "Untying Every kNOT."
YOU:	YOU:	YOU:
YOU:	YOU:	YOU:
YOU:	YOU:	YOU:

So, what are your kNOTS? Sometimes we don't even realize we have them—including the very tight ones. Rest assured, we all have them. Fact is, we've tied most of them around ourselves by way of fear or lack of belief in ourselves, or we have allowed our skeptics to weigh in (many of whom shouldn't even get a vote about anything in our lives)—past or present.

Worse, most of our kNOTS become self-fulling prophecies, which leads to regret. It's a vicious cycle. We move from I can't, I shouldn't, I couldn't to the regret form known as *I should have, I could have, I would have.* Perhaps you know them best as SHOULDA, COULDA, WOULDA! Friends, those are all words of regret. We'll talk more about regret later because it deserves its own chapter.

 Fear is temporary—regrets are forever.

KNOTS – WHY THIS MATTERS TO ME

I wish someone would have told me years ago that we're not the only one who misses out when we allow kNOTS to hold us back. A lot of people—including the people we love most—miss out too. I also never realized how masterful some people—including the ones we're closest to—are at hiding their kNOTS. An exercise in a later chapter may help position you better to discover what kNOT is causing you to miss out, chicken out, or be counted out.

I was born into a very loving home to incredibly young parents. In fact, my parents eloped when they were just teenagers. My dad was from a big family, and my mom was an only child, which she hated. My mom said growing up, my grandmother was super strict. I'll have to take her word for that because I knew her as Gram, who did not have a strict bone in her body. As a grandmother myself now (well, actually, I go by Mimi), I completely get the shift from a strict mother to a whatever-you-want Mimi. Ice cream for breakfast is always on the menu at Mimi's house!

Because my mom did not like being an only child, her heart was set on a large family. My father happily obliged, but I think for "other" reasons. To give you an idea of my dad's sense of humor, he said they produced so many kids because they were too poor to do anything else (wink-wink). So, she got her big family—four babies before she turned 21 years old.

Probably because they were so young, my parents were the perfect combination of young and cool while modeling incredible work ethic and accountability. My dad always had great toys that we all (except my mom) enjoyed together. We had motorcycles, dune buggies, and for our snowy winters, dad built an enormous four-man sled on water skis that he pulled behind his van with the back doors wide open and all of us just inches from falling out. His toys drove my mother crazy for fear of injury. Even the dads of our friends were drawn to participate in my dad's adventures. Just a note here: Today, my dad is approaching 80, and his body and multiple surgery scars remind him daily of his invincible youth. Suffice to say, kNOT was never a word in his vocabulary.

My mom worked full-time in the medical field. In fact, she assisted the same wonderful surgeon for almost 40 years. When the surgeon retired, she was sought-after by other busy surgeons in town. What a confidence booster! I remember thinking, "I want people to fight over hiring me too!"

We had home-cooked meals Sunday through Thursday. I can still see her cooking in her uniform because when you come home to five hungry mouths, there is no time for a wardrobe change. While she wore nursing uniforms every day, she had an eye for fashion and dressed so stylish. I would often sneak into her closet and "borrow" her clothes. Almost every single time I wore something of hers, I ruined it. Sorry, mom!

Growing up, if I had to describe my mom, I would refer to the "I'M A WOMAN" jingle from the '70s Enjoli perfume commercial. It was about an eight-hour perfume for the 24-hour woman (my mom). It went something like this: *"I can bring home the bacon... fry it up in a pan.... and never, never, never, let you forget you're a man—cause I'M A WOMAN, Enjoli!"*

She was an awesome role model. She instilled in me and my three siblings the kind of confidence that with hard work and dedication, we could be, do, or have anything our hearts desired. Neither she nor my dad ever set limits on any of us. They never tied a kNOT around us, nor would they tolerate us trying one around ourselves. So, you can imagine my big surprise.

My Big Surprise, Her Big Secret

What I discovered later in life was a monumental shocker! While my mother was infusing confidence into us, she had none herself. She literally faked it so she would never risk passing on insecurity to her children.

I am still rattled about how such a gifted woman can struggle desperately with insecurity. Was it something in her upbringing? Was having a "strict" mother code for "too restrictive"? Was it being an only child? Was it marrying a wild and crazy teenager? I don't know why. She doesn't know why. To know her, you would struggle to know why because you too would never suspect! Equally, how can someone with such little confidence instill so much confidence in others? I'm hanging my hat on the unconditional love of a mother.

What I've grown to understand is the lack of confidence is a kNOT, a Gordian-level kNOT! I've learned that just because someone appears to have everything doesn't mean they are not or have not tied themselves up in kNOTS.

I'm dedicating this book to the woman who taught me there is no such thing as kNOTS! And in tremendous respect and gratitude to my mom, my prayer is that her story and this book speaks to the hearts and souls of other wonderful people like my mom who have hidden kNOTS that have or are holding them back from living the abundant life God has in store for them. One last thing: It's never too late to start untying!

TODAY: MY kNOTS

My day job is working with large and small healthcare organizations to build systems that drive strategic and sustainable growth. Because I've seen the benefits of it first-hand, I'm a huge proponent of coaching. It helps keep people and organizations on track, accountable, and focused on their desired finish line.

While my job sounds super-focused and strategic, something else you should know about me is that I am a PhD-level productive-procrastinator and suffer severely from Shiny Object Syndrome... SQUIRREL! Add to that the fact that I'm always trying to "fit 50 pounds into a five-pound bag," and you start to get an idea of my personality type.

While I profess to know my limitations, that never seems to stop me *from completely* over-committing and then almost killing myself (and others) to make the "it" happen. Anyone else? *Stay with me.*

I love the saying "readers are leaders" and "learners are earners," which I use to justify all the money I've spent on (sometimes never opened) books, CDs, DVDs, programs, conferences, and e-courses.

I've also spent tons of time (something we can never get back) reading, researching, listening to, subscribing to, or "following" subject-matter-experts in my areas of interest, including speaking, faith, leadership and purpose. *Stay with me.*

I've completed a few nice post-graduate degrees, fellowships, and certificates. Education has certainly positioned me and even opened doors for me, but it is not for everyone and should NEVER be a kNOT to hold anyone back. After all, a lot of wildly successful people didn't have college degrees, people like Steve Jobs, Mark Zuckerberg, and Bill Gates come to mind. *Stay with me.*

I don't share anything about myself to impress you but to impress upon you how many times I've tied the "I'm kNOT ready" kNOT or the "I'm kNOT the expert" kNOT around myself instead of being more like Alexander the Great by drawing my sword and slicing that stinking kNOT in half and *just doing it!*

STARTING WITH OUR OWN FAMILY

You've probably heard these sayings: "doctors are the worst patients," "the carpenter's house is never finished," "the printer has no business cards of his own," "the cobbler's children have no shoes," or "preachers' kids are the wildest." Could these examples lead to kNOTS? Of course, those are platitudes, but the truth is, we and our families are typically the last in line or the first to miss out on—even benefit—from our gifts and talents. Instead, we somehow think the ones we love the most will learn by osmosis or exposure to what we want them to learn, experience, or benefit from what we do or know. If we're not careful, we'll tie kNOTS in the ones we love most—the kNOT that they weren't a priority.

My oldest child Tommy is incredibly smart. In fact, he is the COO of our company now. When he was in school, he was the student you loved to hate because he never had to study for good grades. I guess he got that from his father. When he was a pre-teen and teenager, I would pay him to read a book (is that bad?) and write me a brief summary on what he learned or took away from the book. Typically, they were books I had enjoyed reading, and I thought they would direct him in a positive way. As I think back, I wonder if it was more a case of parental neglect for something important I should have taught him myself. Anyway, on one such occasion, I had him read Stephen Covey's *Seven*

Habits of Highly Successful People. In his summary, he wrote, *"Hey Mom, you should reread this book—especially the part about Habit #3: Putting First Things First!"* OUCH! Well, I knew for sure he read the book!

THE FIRST DAY IS THE WORST DAY

I always say that the first day is the worst day. Think about the first day of a diet, a new training course, or new work-out plan. Once we make it past just the first day, suddenly, motivation is born based on the accomplishment of one day's success.

The reality that motivation *follows* action is completely out of order and feels backward. Who wants to take action and then get motivated? Where's the motivation in that? We are seldom motivated (until a crisis) to do something, especially like identifying and untying one of our own kNOTs. But the motion is the lotion that greases our wheel. The more you move, the easier it gets.

All that to say, to start and keep moving forward, most of us need some form of an accountability partner. If you have any inclination to procrastinate—especially when working on yourself—an accountability partner can have off-the-charts results for you. Accountability partners come by different names. I think you'll recognize and find these accountability partner equations correct.

- Athlete + **Coach** = SUCCESS
- Careerist + **Mentor** = SUCCESS
- Entertainer + **Agent** = SUCCESS
- Speaker/Writer + **Advisor** = SUCCESS
- You + **Friend** = SUCCESS
- Student + **Teacher** = SUCCESS
- Child + **Parent** = SUCCESS
- Anyone + **Jesus** = SUCCESS FOR ETERNITY

If you interview successful people, I guarantee you will hear about others who kept them accountable and moving in a constant forward motion toward success. Having someone walk beside you is the gigantic differentiator in achieving SUCCESS.

I love reading social posts about what successful people consistently do, read, or daily routine, because I always find clues. For years, I went to a dentist who was such a gentle giant. He was super-successful, and I loved having life conversations with him. I remember having a conversation with him once about building a new house. He said when you build a house, the first one won't be the perfect one. The perfect house is the second house you build because you've learned what was successful or not the first time. But what if we can't or don't want to build two houses? How can we get it perfect the first time based on lessons from others?

SUCCESS LEAVES CLUES!

Anytime we start a new program in our company, we research, observe, and if one exists anywhere, we interview other successful organizations and leaders who have gone before us. We first ask, "Would you do it again?" Our next question is, "If you could do it again, what would you change?" The answers are more valuable than gold!

That is why I love the saying, *"success leaves clues"* because it is a proven truth—the same principle applies to failures too. So, why are we so reluctant to search out or reach out to the successful people doing what we're interested in to pick their brains or get direction?

What is most everyone's favorite subject? Themselves! They are their favorite subject, and hopefully, what they're doing is a big part of the reason. Follow the success clues, and then take the initiative and reach out. With that said, I have some dos and don'ts on this process.

DO'S & DONT'S

While working on my own kNOTs, around self-promoting myself for my speaking goals, I took action. If I want to lead millions to discover their why, I need to learn how wildly—successful professional speakers land huge venues and audiences. I started by joining the National Speakers Association (NSA). That is where I met Lois, who is now my speaking-promotion coach. She is a nationally recognized speaker and coach for some mega-famous authors and speakers. I promise you would recognize the names of many of her clients. Lois and I were small-talking about her books and business, when I instantly realized she had exactly what I needed. She wasn't trying to sell me anything, she just shared her journey that led to her consulting (coaching) niche. Her niche was what I was looking for, but I would NEVER have know about her had I not taken that action first to join NSA.

She shared a story about a time she spoke at the National Speakers Association meeting and a reporter from a huge market was in the audience and asked to do a feature story on her. The story ended up on the front page of the paper's business section. The day the story was published, she arrived at her office to a full voice mailbox. There were literally 50 messages from readers who enjoyed the article, and all 50 wanted to meet with her or take her out to lunch or coffee to pick her brain. Many went on to share that they too wanted to be a speaker, yadi-yada.

Because she is so awesomely professional, she returned every single call. She apologized for not having the availability to meet in person but recommended they go to her website and download a tool that would answer many if not all their questions. The tool was only $10—cheaper than lunch, coffee, or the time for either. Guess how many people took her up on that offer? TWO! Only two people acted, taking advantage of an affordable set of answers to their questions. That means only 4 percent acted while the other 96 percent missed a huge opportunity!

The problem? Everyone wants a silver bullet or magic pill vs. doing a little work! Meeting over a meal sounded fun—buying or listening to a program and doing the work and well, that was kNOT sexy!

Now I find or hire accountability partners to get me across the finish line in important areas that I'll share more about later. Before you think you can't afford that luxury, please STOP! You'll be surprised how affordable it is, how much money you can stop spending or wasting and put toward the cost and ultimately the prize in the end. Notice I say "across the finish line." Hiring a coach doesn't mean you don't do the work. Show me a successful athlete whose coach did their hard work. You can't! Same for us.

Let this book be your launching pad or that thrust you need to push you over the finish line.

My prayer is that this book inspires you to not only identify your kNOTS but ignites the bravery to draw on your God-given talents and His power to set you free from the kNOTs holding you back from living the indescribable and undeniable life He designed just for you.

CHAPTER 2
CLARITY OVER COMPLICATION

Imagine what would happen if you started seeing yourself as God sees you.

Every year, I select a word as my go-to word that will help me stay focused on an area where I see opportunities for my own self-improvement. For the last couple of years, I've been stuck on "intentional" because I tend to live life so fast with a focus on what's next, and I neglect what is happening right NOW. A life-changer a few years ago is when my word was "clarity" because without clarity, life gravitates to complication.

If we could see ourselves the way God sees us, we would probably drop dead in shock from all the kNOTS we created for ourselves. I remember when I first learned that God is not a God of chaos and confusion.[1] Knowing that provided the clarity that if my life—or your life—is filled with either chaos or confusion (and it's not just a temporary state), then it's safe to say that's not where God has led us or wants us. That's a good start.

Some people describe their state of chaos and confusion as "complicated." I understand. Chaos builds on chaos until it becomes so loud and confusing that it drowns out any chance of clarity or clear thinking. We often don't really know where it started or how to stop it. So, it's easier to describe it as "complicated"! What I know for certain is that until we can stop long enough to get clarity about our complications, it will be virtually impossible to untie *any* kNOT.

IF YOU'RE FEELING STUCK, SEEK CLARITY

The title and concept of this book has been on my heart for a very long time. Writing a book was never because I could kNOT imagine authoring a whole book! Oddly enough, I write blogs, church messages, speeches, and other content all the time—so why not a book? Most importantly, why not a book that could have a huge impact on tons of people? The thought of it was exhilarating, but how or where would I even start? Who would help me? Do I title it first or last?

So one day, I just started writing, and the who, what, where, and when kNOTS started forming. A book became just unbelievable enough, just overwhelming enough that it drowned out my logic, and so I went to the ole standby kNOT: I'm just too busy! Has that ever happened to you?

What do you have going on that is drowning out your abilities or your ability to get clarity around something you were born to do? What keeps popping in and out of your head or heart that just gives you a bleep of exhilaration or excitement but quickly gets stuck in one of your standby or comfort zone kNOTS?

It is so easy for things to get stuck in kNOTS—sometimes before we even get started—because we often just don't know where to start. Sometimes for me, it's procrastination, but other times, as mentioned above, I legitimately get stuck and quit. There is a name for that.

TOO OFTEN, WHEN WE GET STUCK - WE GET STUPID

When you read "stupid," you either gasped or laughed! But that's been my story more than I care to admit! I write all the time, but I allowed a stupid kNOT to convince me I wasn't an "author." That's what I mean by stupid. It's an ugly word, but I hope the ugliness of it jolts you into action like it did me. What stupid kNOT have you allowed yourself to believe that is holding you back? Is it crystal clear to people you trust, and they've even mentioned you should do "it," but for you, "it" is too far-reaching?

Let me illustrate with an old fable about the guy who was stuck on his rooftop during a big flood. He was praying for help. Soon, a man in a rowboat came by, and the fellow shouted to the man on the roof, "Jump in, I can save you." The stranded guy shouted back, "No, it's okay, I'm praying, and God is going to save me." So the rowboat went on.

Then a motorboat came by. The fellow in the motorboat shouted, "Jump in, I can save you." To this, the stranded man said, "No thanks, I'm praying, and God is going to save me. I have faith." So the motorboat went on.

Then a helicopter came by and the pilot shouted down, "Grab this rope, and I will lift you to safety." To this, the stranded man again replied, "No thanks, I'm praying, and God is going to save me. I have faith." So the helicopter reluctantly flew away.

Soon, the water rose above the rooftop, and the man drowned.

The guy went to Heaven and got the chance to discuss the whole situation with God. He said, "God, I had faith in you, but you didn't save me, you let me drown, and I don't understand why!" To that God replied, "I sent you a rowboat and a motorboat and a helicopter. What more did you expect?"

We expect everything, even answers to our prayers, to be so crystal clear, but that rarely ever happens. But are you seeing what I mean about stuck and stupid here? Maybe I should start referring to stuck *on* stupid as SOS!

How I Started Getting My kNOTS Unstuck

Personally, I finally got fed up with my own SOS. I was also fed up with my start-stuck-stop, then rinse-and-repeat over and over again, just leading to more kNOTS. It was exhausting. Professionally, I fell into a vicious cycle of coaching leaders and organizations by day, which I love, only to run out of steam in my personal life where I should be helping lead the ones I love most. Remember my Habit #3 blunder (First Things Things)—I obviously needed a repeat course. I felt so hypocritical.

I think we all reach a point in our life when we have found ourselves stuck in a "kNOT"-so-ideal situation. Perhaps we're stuck with a mortgage on a house or a loan on a vehicle that no longer has the same luster. In a friendship that has more drama than Jerry Springer meets The Housewives of any Crazy Town. We sometimes feel stuck in an important relationship that used to be so exciting and on fire (wink wink) but is now filled with more strife than spice.

Maybe we're stuck in a job that feels like *Groundhog's Day* (same stuff different day) or *One Flew Over the Cuckoo's Nest* (shouldn't need an explanation). Stuck with debt for things we did not need and do not use. Right about now, I'm envisioning my closet. Sorry, I digress.

We get stuck in habits! Stuck in low self-esteem or self-pity—sometimes so stuck we relocate our entire family to Victimville. Instead of feeling grateful for what we *do have*, we get stuck focusing on what we do kNOT have. Anger issues cause us to get stuck and create huge kNOTs.

 The enemy of success is COMFORT!

A big kNOT is the fear of leaving our comfort zone, even though to come into our calling, we must come out of our comfort zone.

We get stuck in a temporary situation, feeling like life is falling off the rails. Stuck from our lack of planning—direction or vision—riding on a roller-coaster to nowhere.

If we're honest with ourselves—me included—if we're not careful when we are stuck and left to our own fleshly desires and devices, we all land on stupid.

There are so many stuck and stupid stories in human history. We've all heard stories that include presidents, entertainers, athletes, and big organizational and church leaders. If you're human, I bet you too have a stuck and stupid story.

Some of the best SOS stories can be found in the Bible because I'm certain God was trying to make us feel better about all the times we have or are contemplating at this very minute. Thankfully, more than the SOS stories are thousands of promises about how God can and will rescue us when we're stuck, and yes—even after stupidity strikes.

There is a well-known SOS story about a married couple Abraham and Sarah. They were both in their late 80s, and suffice to say way past their prime child-bearing years. Even though they were never able to have children, God promised Abraham he would be the father of many nations. Abraham was much more optimistic than Sarah. In fact, as any woman in her late 80s would do, Sarah laughed to herself when Abraham gave her the news that she would conceive and give birth. Sarah could kNOT conceive or believe such an idea was possible—even knowing the source!

I need to pause here and remember how easy it is to look at this story from the outside and think, *"Sarah, good grief. If God said it, just relax, He'll make it happen!"* Sarah was a very intelligent woman, but spoiler alert, she got impatient, which led to her getting stuck and very stupid. Wait until you read what she did!

Sarah devised a plan to get the ball rolling. She had her husband Abraham sleep with her maid to get another woman pregnant. And you don't have to be a rocket scientist to know how she immediately felt about the other woman—yeah, the one who slept with her husband. Shocker, Sarah got jealous. She got mean and possessive. It only got worse as Sarah watched it all play out. In fact, Sarah ended up forcing Abraham to send the maid and her child packing. Not into a nice apartment in another town, no, she and her son were sent out to the desert!

Just as God promised, Abraham and Sarah did conceive a son of their own, and his name was Isaac. But Sarah's stupidity caused a lot of undue pain and suffering instead of patiently waiting on God's promise. Wonder how many times we're guilty of the same?

WHEN THE STUCK ON STUPID CYCLE SEEMS TO HAVE NO END

It doesn't matter how high-ranking you are, if you're a human, you will have a few SOS stories. What you don't want is a vicious cycle of SOS stories like the true story about a legendary king and born warrior. His name was David, and long before he became king, he was the young shepherd boy, who with his slingshot, took out lions and bears who attempted to eat his animals. Those perfected skills led to him taking out a giant warrior named Goliath with the same slingshot.

Fast forward to the adult version of King David. In those times, kings went into battle with their armies. When the story picks up, David has become King, and for some reason, he was sitting the current battle out. At home one night, he couldn't sleep, got bored (stuck), and went out onto his roof balcony. Looking out over his land, he spotted a beautiful woman bathing in her home. Yes, King David turned into Peeping Tom! Here comes the stupid.

He called his servant in and asked about the woman. His servant informed him she was the wife of one of his military leaders who was currently AWAY fighting in King David's army—the very place David should have been too!

Instead of accepting she was a married woman, he starts turning up his **STUPID** meter, sends for her, and sleeps with her. Stuck and stupid.

As stupid luck would have it, she later sends him a note that she is pregnant. Ooops—back to stuck!

He concocts a plan. He calls her husband out of battle for a meeting. It was there - during David's first job - that he perfected the skills that served him well, starting with using the same slingshot to do what no other experienced soldier could. He took out Goliath - the nasty giant enemy warrior. I bet you've heard that story.

After meeting and getting an update from the battle zone, David thanked him for his service and gifted him with a night at home to make love to his wife before going back to battle. But the next morning, David was notified that the man didn't go home but instead slept in the servant's quarter.

Why didn't he go home to his wife? Because, he said, there was no way he would enjoy a normal life while his troops slept in tents on the battlefield. His exact words were, "As surely as you live, I will not do such a thing!" So David moved to Plan B: getting the husband drunk, thinking he would be more relaxed and open to going home to his wife, temporarily forgetting about his comrades. Nope, being a man of honor, he didn't go to his wife again.

Now David was super-duper-stuck! He actually blew the top off the stupid meter up with his unimaginable next move.

In the morning, David wrote a letter and sent it back to the battlefield with the husband. In it, he wrote, "Put him out in front where the fighting is fiercest. Then withdraw from him so he will be struck down and die."

Stuck and stupid, stuck and stupid, stuck and SUPER STUPID!

CLARITY GETS US UNSTUCK

In the movie *Moneyball* with Brad Pitt and Jonah Hill, Pitt plays Billy Beane, the general manager for the Oakland A's, and Jonah plays his Yale-trained statistician.

It's a true story about how together, they were able to take a financially broke and nearly last-place team to a championship game.

BUT while still "STUCK" *in last place*, Beane called his team of scouts and coaches together and asked them if they knew WHY the team was stuck. He called it "the problem," and he asked them all, "What's the problem?"

They were all super put off by his question. (That's a sign people don't really know the answer.)

So, each of them shared their own arrogant answer to the problem, and after each answer, Beane shrieked "NOPE, NAH, NOOOO, BONK!" Beane finally told them the problem: the WHY they were... STUCK.

I won't spoil the movie, but the moral of the story was, once the problem—the reason they were stuck—was defined, it was a game changer (no pun intended) for the Oakland A's. Watch the movie; it's good! It was a great illustration of being stuck and how not until they found clarity did they get "UNSTUCK." Things were never going to change or improve until they accepted reality. Some of the team quit. Some were fired. Some owned it and made it happen!

Sometimes we don't even realize we're stuck, which means we might not even feel the drift into the stupid lane.

In those cases, perhaps it's because we won't or don't stop the bus long enough to even consider that we're stuck, or worse, we've just learned to accept stuck as our way of life. It doesn't have to be that way!

THE COMPLICATED RISKS

I know what you're thinking. Well, those are great stories, Tammy, but my stuck situation is much more complicated! Ah yes, of course it is... STUPID ME.

If you Google the word "complication," you'll find the number of times people die from complications. More people die NOT from what happened to them, like surgery, injury, or illness, but from their "complications."

COMMON THINGS THAT HAPPEN TO COVER UP STUCK:

- We tie ourselves up in our own excuses: *It's complicated, I didn't know, I deserve it.*
- We run back to "the familiar," even if it's wrong or **STUPID**.
- We slide back into our comfort zone.
- We start playing head games with ourselves.
- Complication is a kNOT. Don't be a complication statistic!

CHAPTER 3

HEAD OR HEART CONDITION

Guard your heart above all else, for it determines the course of your life.[2]

Wait, what's the problem? YOU! And Me! We really are our biggest problem! Oh, how I know it's so much easier to play the blame game, pointing the finger at something or someone else. But if we're really honest with ourselves, we would admit that most of our kNOTS are self-conceived and self-inflicted. Yep, we invent them; we bind them and store them nicely inside for easy access.

Before we can untie any kNOT, we must first figure out **why** it exists. Until then, we won't discover the root to be able to find the solution or way to untie the kNot to be set free.

Are our kNOTS due to a head or a heart condition? The short answer is both because both organs are so powerful. Left to their own devices, *together*, they can literally fashion a Gordian-sized kNOT situation.

Our Paradigm Can Tie Huge kNOTs

We all have our own paradigms—our lens or perspective, the way we see things based on our beliefs, experiences, sometimes even our moods. My all-time favorite story about paradigms is about a businessman who likes to unwind on weekends by taking his fast sports car out for a spin.

One such Saturday, he was out for a drive and approaching a sharp turn, and out of nowhere, a car came around veering out of control. He quickly pulled over, and as the car passed, the driver yelled "PIG!" He was so caught off guard hearing a stranger call him a name, he responded quickly with "You cow!" He was thinking "Lady, you're the one driving out of control." But he instantly felt vindicated because she called him a name and he was able to react and even the score quickly! Feeling great, he pulled back on the road, charged around the corner, and ran right into the PIG!

What was meant to be a warning he heard as a THREAT. What was an "opportunity" to protect him and his "beloved" sports car instead led to a CRASH! Paradigms are powerful kNOT-binding agents.

THE POWER OF THE HEART

My sister Andrea is an organ donor. She successfully donated a kidney to her son, my nephew Nathan. They live states apart, so after discharge, Andrea stayed with me for a couple of additional recovery weeks. We spent two weeks binge-watching Downton Abbey—suffice it to say she was an extremely easy patient!

In preparation for the transplant, our entire family did a ton of research on organ transplantation. During my research of the dos and don'ts around kidney transplantation, I ran across many heart-warming stories. As it turns out, the best stories were not about kidney transplant patients but about heart transplantation patients. Unlike Andrea and Nathan's story, to get a heart, the donor has died, bringing a whole new level of emotion to the story.

What intrigued me the most about heart transplant recipients was more than just how their health changed after the surgery. The stories revealed how the recipients developed qualities and interests of their donors. It was insanely fascinating!

One patient whose music preference was straight up rock-n-roll developed his donor's interest and passion for classical music. Another acquired a new taste and craving for Mexican food from their donor who loved Mexican food. One young patient woke up from surgery, and when his mom asked how he felt, he immediately responded, "Everything is copacetic." The child had never heard or used that term before his surgery. But later, the parents discovered the term was frequently used by his donor when she and her husband made up after an argument, indicating all was well. That's pretty darn copacetic!

But by far, my favorite story was the young girl who received a heart from a murdered child. The murder case was unsolved. This young girl who received the heart kept having dreams about the murder. The dreams were so vivid that she was able to share specific details that led to the case being solved and the murderer convicted!

 The heart is powerful.

Thankfully, most of us will never experience an organ transplant, but we all have stories of the power of the heart trumping the wisdom of the head.

I recall reading about a survey conducted on 1,500 people regarding their career path choice. The answers were not surprising:

Group A (83 percent) went with their head and selected a career that provided the best pay, delaying the pursuit of their dream job until after they made money.

Group B (17 percent) selected a career doing what they love first, delaying the pursuit of money for later.

What was surprising is that 20 years later, the same group was surveyed, and 101 of the 1,500 were millionaires. But wait. Almost all (99 percent) or 100 of the 101 were from Group B, the group that went with their heart and pursued something they loved over the pursuit of money.

Personally, I fell into group A. I delayed college to go after the money. I wasn't a stellar student and really only enjoyed the socialization part of school, not the actual learning or schoolwork. While others went off to college, I went off to work. Little did I know, college would have been high school fun on steroids! It wasn't even for a career; it was just for the money. I thought money was the answer to the pursuit of success. It wasn't until after I married and had my first child that I realized to reach my dream, I needed a college education.

This is not a judgement call on anyone, but to illustrate, I followed my head and sacrificed much more later. Going to college later while working a full-time job with a husband and child is not a ton of fun! They sacrificed as much as I did.

As I write this, my 4.0 GPA, honor-student granddaughter (finally) selected a university. She had many options from full-ride academic scholarships with in-state universities to small or no academic tuition reductions at out-of-state universities. Her parents worked out a formula where she would be responsible for a portion of the tuition costs, but any scholarship monies would be applied to her portion. Conventional wisdom suggests she would select a university that provides the best tuition discount or scholarship to reduce her portion of costs. Nope, not so much. She selected an out-of-state college that did not provide her with any academic tuition reductions. Since location and climate was clearly important to her, it appeared she was making her decision based only on her heart. Knowing she wants a good education—and is willing to pay for a part of it—she went with a university in a warm climate. So watch out, Arizona—here she comes!

Some of us have never considered the power our hearts hold. Our hearts have the power to think, to speak, and to influence. Our hearts bind some of our strongest kNOTS. There is a lot written about the power and transparency of our heart. The Bible is so clear, and it was Jesus who said, *"The good person out of the good treasure of the heart produces good, and the evil person out of evil treasure produces evil; for it is out of the abundance of the heart that the mouth speaks"* (Luke 6:45).

I remember saying something snarky to my husband during an argument. He replied by informing me what I was thinking. Outraged, I reminded him that he was not a mind-reader and had no idea what I was feeling or thinking. He said he didn't have to be a mind-reader, my words revealed what was in my heart.

While luckily, most of us will never need a heart transplant, all of us have an Olympic-level kNOT-tying heart condition. Left unchecked, our hearts can tie the most paralyzing, life-limiting, dream-smashing kNOTs.

Just so I didn't leave anything to chance, what is the biggest sign of a kNOT-tying heart condition? Our mouth and actions! The Book of Wisdom (Proverbs 23:7) tells us that "For as a man thinks in his heart... so he is." So there you have it, you and I really do have the power within our own hearts to live a kNOT-free life.

Anyone's heart can harden by pride, sin, disbelief, or disappointments. It can affect the way we see God's love and goodness. These are kNOTs that keep us from embracing God's gifts of love, grace, and mercy. They can change the way we see others and send us down a wrong path.

This is a perfect time to pause and ask God to examine the wellness of your heart. Just pray, *"Lord, is there anything, anyone, in my life causing my heart to be hardened?"* Ask Him to *give you a heart that is tender and moldable. To soften any place that has become calloused because of pride, sin, unbelief or disappointments.* Ask him *to give you a heart like His.* He will show up, giving us the opportunity to come clean with our heat-hardening struggles and be molded into a heart like His.

CHAPTER 4

KNOWING THE END OF THE STORY

The days are long, but the years are short.

This might be my favorite chapter because of the heart-stopping, mind-blowing "what if" questions. I hope you will take the time to stop, reflect, and answer each of them.

✤ *What if... the greatest story ever told had you as the main character?*

How would that story go? Who would it include in the story? How would the story end?

✤ *What if... you were given the opportunity to do/ become something you knew you couldn't fail at?*

Basically, what would you do if you *knew the end of the story* was a success? Well, what would you do?

Isn't it funny how much we can get done—at home or work—just before we leave for vacation? We get a sense of urgency like no other time during the year. Why can't we live everyday with that same sense? We've all heard songs or stories about the sense of urgency that happens to those who are told they don't have long to live.

Here is another life-critical "what if?" that helps to appreciate a real sense of urgency.

✤ *What if... you only had 30 days to live?*

List the things you would do in your last 30 days. Go ahead, what would you do? Set a timer for five minutes (it probably won't take the entire five to complete). Ready, set, go.

I use this question in one of my training courses, and not one time from hundreds of people have I ever heard anyone say anything about wrapping things up at work. In fact, no one has ever listed anything about work. It's amazing how much we miss out on because of mixed-up priorities, but maybe that's just me.

THE LAW OF GRAVITY: WHAT GOES UP MUST COME DOWN

I've always loved being a career woman. I wanted to be a superwoman like my mom. For 21 years, I worked for a large, multi-hospital health system in the Midwest. Right out of high school, I started in an entry-level position at one of the hospitals. I only got that job because of the relationships my mom had formed through her work with the hospital. I worked hard, and during my third year, I won Employee of the Year. I felt like I won Miss America and didn't even know I was qualified! That motivated me to work even harder. Recognition often goes so much further than money.

Thankfully, the work ethic and no-job-is-beneath-me mentality that I saw modeled by my parents paid off, and helped me climb the corporate ladder. Side note: Employers (including me) look for drive more than degrees. "Hard work pays off" is NOT just a cliché! I refer to it as having a fire in your belly.

 Drive Trumps Degree

For 21 years, I got unbelievable exposure, experience, and benefits, including having my entire undergraduate education funded. Just for the record, it is my opinion that experience is always the best training camp. Get it at a well-known organization, and it becomes the very BEST. The education is kind of the Good Housekeeping seal of approval. I learned more in the trenches than I ever learned in a classroom, but as in many industries, the education or degree is what opens the next door to advancement. College was a means to an end for me. I will say going to college after I found my career niche was a million times easier than it would have been going to college before I had a clue what I wanted to do. I was able to select classes that applied to my specific area of interest. My undergraduate degree is in marketing.

Since I've only ever worked in healthcare, I don't have a good measuring stick for other industries. What I know is healthcare has no bounds, and you must be a master juggler to survive the ever-changing demands. I guess that's because it's a 24/7/365 business, helping people in their best and worst times, from the beginning of life to the end with a whole lot in the middle. It takes a lot of players and a lot of planning to make healthcare work. It NEVER stops changing. That's for another book. One of the upsides of healthcare is the endless career options. You can be a clinician of any kind, a researcher, a bean counter, an attorney, a lobbyist, an IT guru, an insurance specialist, a tradesman, a cook, a housekeeper, a gardener, a sales rep, and so many other options. Each one makes a difference in the lives of the patients, families and communities we serve.

I've always had a habit of doing things fast but, many times backwards. I got married right out of high school, not because I had to, but because I didn't want to wait. I got a job before going to college because I wanted to start making money—fast. I had kids then started college so I could climb higher and make more money. My career became everyone's priority. I lived to work, not worked to live. That puts a strain on any family—if not immediately, it happens eventually.

As my career took off, my personal life started to crumble. I divorced, not just because of my work, but it played a part. When we divorced, I didn't ask for money, I just asked for help with the kids so I could keep the same pace. While being a single parent and working isn't easy, I chose not to slow down; instead, I worked even harder. I thought I was kNOT going to let being a single parent handicap me. I was superwoman. I'm embarrassed to say that my kids paid a price for my selfish choice.

Often, I would leave in the dark and come home after dark. This was before high-speed internet, and so I could keep up with the enormous amount of emails, the health system installed a T-1 line in my home. I was never out of touch and could communicate at the speed of light. I sent emails from 3 a.m. to 5 a.m. then showered and went off to work.

I remember one evening, I was at a dinner meeting in the city, and I received a call from my kids that the tornado whistles were blowing and "it looked really bad outside." They were scared, and I was way too far away to help them. I remember turning to the executives I was with and told them what was happening, and it was like I told them my kids saw a birdie out the window and just wanted to call and tell me. The tornado didn't hit anywhere near them, but for God's sake—what if?

It wasn't long after that night when I again arrived home late. I remember the fireplace was going, and my teenage son had left a plate of dinner out for me. It felt so normal, until he dropped the bomb. He said, "Hey mom, I think we're going to go live with dad." In his sweet way, he justified the decision because I was so busy at work, could never be home, etc. I heard nothing but my heart exploding.

 What does success matter if I sacrifice what matters most?

The next day, I called my leader about stepping down. She told me there was no going back: once the boss, always the boss. So I called Human Resources to research my options. I read all the relevant policies myself. I knew that one of the health centers under my leadership had an opening for an administrator. The top of the position's pay scale was close to the bottom of my pay scale—I'll tell you later about policies you should understand. I knew it was a challenging enough role in a large center that I felt I could make an impact. I could even propose hanging on to a couple of well-managed sites to try and keep most of my compensation. More importantly, it would support me working less and getting home before dark every night, but most of all, it would support me being a better mom. I untied my superwoman kNOT and stepped down.

 I untied my superwoman kNOT and stepped down.

Side note that may be of help to someone: Within large organizations, there are generally compensation policies for existing employees in terms of how much a salary can increase at one time. Unfortunately, it works against employees during internal job advancements. It's such a disservice to the advancement of existing employees, and it's why for the same position, external candidates often start at a higher salary than an existing employee.

For example, if you're currently in a $25 an hour position and the new position is a $40 per hour position, with a salary cap policy of 25 percent (which is high) the most you could make is $31.25 per hour, while an outsider would get the $40 per hour rate. When I stepped down, they did a national search for my replacement. Her salary was substantially more than mine. I had been there 17 years and fell under the "policy" caps—except it was overridden one time for me. Another note: Any policy can be amended on a case-by-case basis. Challenge it every time! Untie someone's kNOT!

Luckily, what I discovered in my research was the same policy applies to a salary decrease. So, I stepped down, and my base salary did not change. I lost my executive bonus package, but bonuses are never guaranteed. While the bonus "potential" had always resulted in a chunk of money, the base compensation was what I relied on or needed to stay financially whole.

Right Place, Right Time

In my personal and professional life, I have experienced or witnessed countless "in the right place at the right time" moments. Life is a contact sport! I don't believe in coincidence—I believe in divine orchestration. So, every time it happens, I give a quick thanks to God for orchestrating the contact. Had I not stepped down, I would not have been in the position for what came next.

 Life is a contact sport.

I loved the shift, or better said, *the gift* of my new position. Instead of 22 sites, I just had one big one! The health center was like a hospital without beds. It had all the other services (lab, radiology, pharmacy, eye care, procedural suites) and a large multi-specialty group of physicians and advanced practitioners. It was so much more hands-on, and it was so rewarding to take something from concept to implementation. It literally felt like I jumped off a run-away high-speed locomotive onto a high-class cruise ship. But the most important improvement was that I could be a better, more engaged mom. My personal life started to get back on track. I even remarried a wonderful man and long-time friend. Things were lining up.

One of the busiest departments within the health center was experiencing a patient bottleneck problem. With high patient volumes, they couldn't configure a patient flow process that worked. The nursing manager asked if I would meet with a consultant friend of hers who might be able to help. She must have way oversold my status within the organization because her friend brought an entourage, including the president of the consulting firm, perhaps thinking I was the door to the entire health system.

In a casual conversation with the consultants, I learned they had many offices around the country, including in San Antonio, Texas. That caught my attention because my in-laws live in San Antonio, and I knew my husband would love to relocate there someday. I casually mentioned that if an executive position opened in the future, I'd love to hear about it.

Fast forward less than a year later; I received a call from the firm's president informing me of an open position. It was not just any position but the first-time-ever kind of position. It was the first time in history a medical school faculty plan (700 physicians) ever outsourced their entire management team. The consulting firm landed this unbelievable deal! I was identified for the COO position.

It was the easiest process I had ever experienced, so I just knew it was meant to be! And candidly, I knew one of two things would happen. Either I would fall flat on my face, or they would write textbooks about me. I was banking (literally) on the latter and accepted the job. I spent the next two months transitioning out and celebrating 21 awesome years.

Had I not stepped down, I never would have been positioned for this opportunity.

THE MOVING VAN

My entire life, I had lived within the same ten-mile radius – so heading 1,000 miles away was both scary and exciting. The movers came and loaded up all our belongings into an 18-wheeler and headed to Texas. We were a day behind in our cars. My in-laws found a nice house in their neighborhood for us to lease. The mantra "everything is bigger in Texas" is so true. The rooms (especially the bedrooms, bathrooms, and closets) are supersized! I was in love! My husband planned to get us settled in then return to Illinois to sell our home and wrap up a commercial construction project he was leading. That took two years!

The afternoon before we left, I was heading home from the store with our travel snacks and got a call on my cell phone from the consulting firm. They told me the deal with the university had fallen through. My words, not theirs. Their words were, "the final contract wasn't signed as planned, but we're still good. We just wanted to inform you in case you heard anything though the rumor mill (i.e., newspaper)." They were confident that it would be back on schedule soon.

BACK TO MY "WHAT IF" GAME

Without a final contract, I wondered what that meant for me. So I asked, "what if" the contract doesn't get signed. They assured me they had tons of other business. I asked for examples, after all I did just quit a job of 21 years and everything I owned was in a moving truck headed to Texas. They mentioned they were looking at a lot of compliance consulting. At the time, the new patient privacy and security compliance laws known as HIPAA for Health Insurance Portability and Accountability Act was just being introduced. Please note here, you might as well pluck my fingernails out one by one rather than ask me to do anything remotely connected to compliance. I did kNOT do compliance! I arrogantly responded, "I hire people to do that!" They asked if they could delay my start date just by a week to work through the details with the university. Off to Texas we went.

THANK GOD FOR PRIVACY LAWS

Turns out, if it weren't for HIPAA, we would not have eaten for a year. We arrived in Texas, unloaded and instantly fell in love with all things Texas. I started the new job a week later and immediately read the tea leaves. Based on what the university was saying, I knew the deal was over. I worked with academia in my health system position, and the words they used were fancy academic talk for "no deal." The firm was in denial, so since there were 40 hospitals in the market, I just started networking. I would literally call people who held similar positions to the one I left behind and say, "Hey, can we meet?" It just so happens the county medical society was the fourth or fifth largest in the nation, so I reached out to them too. And I waited. I also started studying the Federal Register to learn what I could about HIPAA laws. I entered the untie-my-kNOT or starve phase.

As soon as I removed that kNOT, my mindset changed. Oddly enough, I found the HIPAA regulations super interesting mainly because lawmakers—not healthcare professionals—wrote the laws on one very wrong assumption. They assumed doctors, nurses, and all other healthcare professionals didn't care about patient privacy. Their "wrong" assumption got my attention. The regulations were so convoluted, further over-complicating what doctors needed to do to be in compliance with the new laws. Only then was I "in it to win it" for a healthcare industry that had and will always care about patient privacy. Oh yeah, I also enrolled in graduate school because San Antonio has one of the best executive healthcare graduate programs in the country. That helped later with connections for business, starting with the Executive Director of the Medical Society who I later discovered was an alumnus.

We joined an awesome non-denominational Christian church. My youngest loved the youth program so much that she would literally cry if I tried to skip church! I laugh thinking God has such a good sense of humor using my child to get me to attend church regularly. The church was so organized and friendly that I got plugged in right away by signing up to volunteer.

I remember working in the coffee shop where my teenager-boss taught me to say excuse me vs. please move! I worked in the office making and sorting copies. I had obviously gotten too big for my britches, and God had a funny way of humbling me! All jokes aside, if you're ever in San Antonio, please look up Summit Christian Center—it is amazing! The practical learning with timely and relevant Bible truth weaved throughout makes it so relatable for everyone. I met my corporate accountant at church, and while we've been back in Illinois for years now, he's still my accountant from Texas.

While my husband wasn't there yet, thankfully all my in-laws, including cousins, lived in the same subdivision, so we had a great support system. The elementary school was at the edge of our subdivision within walking distance from any of our houses.

After just under a month, the management deal officially fell through with the university. I remember being at home one afternoon meeting the cable guy when I had "the job renegotiation call" with the president of the firm. I was walking around the house, splitting my attention between directing the cable guy on television locations and having my job option conversation with the president.

She proceeded to offer me the position of running their local firm or moving to somewhere in southern Texas to manage a large physician group. I can't remember the name of the town, but I do remember repeating the name of the town, just thinking out loud, and the cable guy heard me and quickly came crawling out from behind our entertainment center waving his hands and shaking his head, "NO NO!" I told the president I would talk to my husband that evening and get back to her.

When I hung up, the cable guy said, "Ma'am I don't know you and have only been in your house for a few minutes, but what I do know is you would not fit well in that town." He said among other things, they have chickens for pets, loose in their front yards. He said, "I just don't see you fitting in that environment." I laughed and agreed. That night, I talked to my husband about the offer to run the firm. Without hesitation, he said, "If you're going to run any firm, it's going to be your own firm." And that night, Tiller-Hewitt HealthCare Strategies was born. That had never ever crossed my mind. I did kNOT have my husband's kind of entrepreneur spirit.

 Good things happened every time a kNOT was untied!

The next day, I quit the firm, cashed out my 401k, and got to work. With no income on my end, that decision forced my husband to stay working in Illinois. The house finally sold, which helped us financially. To help more, he literally rented and moved into a roach-infested trailer. They apparently weren't there when he signed the lease, but shortly after, the neighbor across the street set off a bug-bomb and sent all the roaches running right into his trailer. Every night when we talked, he was so positive, encouraging me to keep pounding the pavement, promising me that people just didn't know they needed me ... yet!

I spent my days selling Tiller-Hewitt, doing homework and networking wherever and with whomever I could. By night, I worked on developing or tweaking my program offerings. We now fondly refer to that process as "building the plane while we fly it." Ultimately, my goal was to work with hospitals and health systems, but that sales cycle is long because hospitals are large and bureaucratic. So, in the short term, I did consulting with physician groups and did sales for the Medical Society.

I remember an early sales trip to Kansas City to call on a health system. That morning from the hotel, I checked the balance of our savings account, and it was at ZERO! I remember not knowing what else to do but pray. Stupid me—I saved praying for my last act instead of my first. I didn't hear God's voice audibly, but I did feel in my heart Him saying, *"It's about time you trust Me!"* Again, that superwoman kNOT held me back.

Guess how I paid bills the first year? Yes, you guessed it, compliance! On none other than HIPAA consulting. I thank God for not holding my earlier arrogance against me. Being broke brought a whole new level of humility.

Shortly after that Kansas City trip, I landed my first hospital client. The icing on the cake was it was with a local health system. I didn't even have to travel! I never looked back.

And those were some of my biggest personal and professional kNOT stories. We just never know what we'll gain when we start untying kNOTS. I had no idea of all the kNOTS I had picked up until God had to pull the rug out. But what I gained would have been humanly impossible to do.

THE BUCKET LIST

Do you have a bucket list? That is a list of things you want to do before you "kick the bucket." I have one and coach others to create them as well. It's much different and bigger than a "things to do" list. My bucket list includes writing a book, giving a TED Talk, traveling across the country in a luxury RV, spending one month in a vacation spot where I can see and visit beautiful mountains AND the ocean, and seeing the Northern Lights. What about you—what is on your bucket list?

There is an awesome movie titled *The Bucket List* with Jack Nicholson and Morgan Freeman. They meet as terminally ill patients sharing a hospital room. Nicholson plays a billionaire business tycoon (who happens to own the hospital), and Freeman plays a scholarly mechanic. Freeman is forced to endure Nicholson's arrogance and anger resulting from having to share a room. Ironically, the reason Nicholson could not have his own room is because of a "two beds to a room—no exception" mandate he established - as a greedy business mogul. But he admitted in one of his rants that the mandate was made "before he got sick."

They had nothing in common until both were given a terminal diagnosis on the same day. This created an immediate bond, and a deep friendship ensued. They decided to venture out together, working off a combined bucket list. It's a great movie. I've watched it countless times. The problem with a bucket list is they're typically made too late—like after a catastrophic diagnosis or event. In the movie, bored in his hospital bed, Freeman started writing his bucket list, but once he received his terminal diagnosis, he tore it up and threw it on the floor. I assume he thought it was too late.

Don't tie a kNOT around life. It's not too late! It's not too early. You're not too old. You're not too young. You're not too small. You're not too large. Did I cover everyone?

If you're a person of faith, you know God's promise of life-everlasting with Him when we acknowledge Jesus came to earth for one reason, to rescue us. Our eternal story has been written. But God wants us to live an abundant kNOT-free life on planet earth too! Let's commit to living with a greater sense of urgency—the days go slow, but the years fly by.

ALL ABOARD

Years ago, before transatlantic flight was common, a man wanted to travel to the United States from Europe. The man worked hard, saved every extra penny he could, and finally had just enough money to purchase a ticket aboard a cruise ship. The trip at that time required about two or three weeks to cross the ocean. He went out and bought a suitcase and filled it full of cheese and crackers. That's all he could afford.

Once on board, all the other passengers went to the large, ornate dining room to eat their gourmet meals. Meanwhile, the poor man would go over in the corner and eat his cheese and crackers. This went on day after day. He could smell the delicious food being served in the dining room. He heard the other passengers speak of it in glowing terms as they rubbed their bellies and complained about how full they were and how they would have to go on a diet after this trip. The poor traveler wanted to join the other guests in the dining room, but he had no extra money. Sometimes he'd lie awake at night, dreaming of the sumptuous meals the other guests described.

Toward the end of the trip, another man came up to him and said, "Sir, I can't help but notice that you are always over there eating those cheese and crackers at mealtimes. Why don't you come into the banquet hall and eat with us?"

The traveler's face flushed with embarrassment. "Well, to tell you the truth, I had only enough money to buy the ticket. I don't have any extra money to purchase fancy meals."

The other passenger raised his eyebrows in surprise. He shook his head and said, "Sir, don't you realize the meals are included in the price of the ticket? Your meals have already been paid for!"

God has prepared a fabulous banquet for you.

When I heard this story, I couldn't help but think of how many people are like that naive traveler. They are missing out on God's best because they don't realize that the good things in life have already been paid for. They may be on their way to heaven, but they don't know what has been included in the price of their ticket.

Every moment that we go around forgetting that "the harvest is plentiful," instead we eat more cheese and crackers. Every time we shrink back and say, "Well I can kNOT do it; I do kNOT have what it takes," we're eating more cheese and crackers. Every time we go around full of fear, worry, and anxiety or we are uptight about something, we're over there eating more cheese and crackers. Friend, I don't know about you, but I'm tired of those cheese and crackers! It's time to step up to God's table.

God has prepared a fabulous banquet for you, complete with every good thing imaginable. And it has already been paid for. God has everything you need there—joy, forgiveness, restoration, peace, healing—whatever you need, it's waiting for you at God's banquet table if you'll pull up your chair and take the place He has prepared for you.

CHAPTER 5
REGRET-PROOF

Cornell University did a research project called The Legacy Project. The project researchers asked 1,200 elder Americans to share their biggest regrets in life. They were sure they would hear regrets like marital affairs, bad business deals, addictions, etc. But what they heard was: *I wish I hadn't spent so much of my life worrying.*

 Worry turns into a big ugly Gordian kNOT for certain.

Over and over, as the 1,200 elders in the Legacy Project reflected on their lives, they shared versions of, *"I would have spent less time worrying"* and, *"I regret that I worried so much about everything."* From the vantage point of late life, many people felt that if they were given a single "do-over" in life, they would like to have all the time back they spent worrying. Going a step farther, they said getting that time alone back would be a substantial extension to their life. That project is one of those gifts in life that has already been paid for—I hope you open it!

Why is excessive worry such a big regret? Because *worry wastes a very limited and precious lifetime.* We always think we have plenty of time left, but the cliché *life is short* is real. The days do often go slow, but the years fly by. The oldest Americans tell us to stop torturing ourselves over outcomes that may never come to pass.

 "Of all the words of mice and men, the saddest are, 'It might have been.'"

–Kurt Vonnegut

The end of that quote sums up regret in just four words: "what might have been." The truth is, regret comes into play from what we didn't do—those things that fall into the missed-out or chickened-out categories. Sadly but most likely, it is a result of a choice—our own choice.

Dear Younger Me

Have you ever wished you could step back in time and tap yourself on the shoulder and whisper, *"Hey, don't do that! Seriously, don't do that!"* Maybe yours would be, *"Don't say that or don't eat that,"* or how about, *"Don't drink that, you know what happens when you drink that stuff!"*

I was part of a women's conference, and in pre-taping for a session, I interviewed a multigenerational group of women and asked the number one thing they would advise their younger self. They unanimously answered, "STOP WORRYING ABOUT STUFF!" Including what people thought about them or said about them. Are you seeing a theme here?

If you could tap your younger self on the shoulder, what would you say? I love the lyrics from the song titled "Dear Younger Me" by MercyMe. It's a powerful message from an older version of the artist to his younger self wondering if he knew then (younger self) what he knew now, how much would it change. It's a super thought-provoking song.

The Truth About Worry

Research shows over 90 percent of what we worry about *NEVER EVEN HAPPENS*. Further research found the key characteristic of worry is that it takes place in the absence of actual stressors; that is, we worry when there is literally nothing concrete to worry about! This is why a critically important strategy for regret reduction, according to the elders studied, is to spend time on concrete problem-solving (real stuff) and drastically eliminate time spent worrying (kNOTs we tie).

Worry is a lie we tell ourselves.

The antidote for worry is gratitude. We have far more to be grateful for than to worry about. Let's answer another *what if* question. What if... you woke up tomorrow and all you had left were the things you thanked God for yesterday?

YOUR REGRETS

How would you answer the Legacy Project question about regrets when looking back on your life? Do you know where the wealthiest places on planet earth are found?

Contrary to popular belief, the wealthiest places on planet earth are *not* the oil fields of the Middle East or the gold and diamond mines of South Africa. The wealthiest places on planet earth are cemeteries! Yes, cemeteries.

Buried in those cemeteries are books never written, dreams never to be fulfilled, ideas never spoken. Cemeteries are repositories for visions that never became realities.

Don't take anything to grave with YOU, especially regrets! You think you've drifted out to the deep end too far. Wrong! God will use your drift into the deep end to help others who are out there and don't know Him! Don't die full of good intentions! Don't check out before you show up in this life (see TammyTillerHewitt.com to watch a Discover Your Why video).

In the movie *Last Holiday*, Queen Latifah plays a humble store assistant who is told that she has a rare brain condition with only a few weeks to live. She cashes out her savings and heads off to Europe, moving into a luxury hotel. That death sentence fired up her sense of urgency! After getting a taste of living an "all out" life, she discovers the terminal diagnosis was incorrect. But she did get a taste and a second chance. The experience changed the trajectory of her life.

Most people are so passive about life—letting the days come and go, weekly routines bleed over to monthly routines—rinse and repeat.

Go Deep

I heard the international speaker, author, and leader Bishop TJ Jakes confess that his biggest regret was that he didn't go deeper. He is an international success, and he didn't believe in himself enough to go deeper. That's a kNOT and a form of chickening out! Will you regret not going deeper? Some suggest that what God has for **EACH OF US is in the deep water.** Now that's deep, right?

The 90/80 Rule

If one of your dreams is to start your own business, let me give you some scary but encouraging stats. Ninety percent of new businesses fail, **BUT** 90 percent of second businesses **succeed**. The sad reality is 80 percent of entrepreneurs fail to try a second time. Too often, we take it as a personal failure. We must remember that failure is an event, not a person. If it's your dream, don't kNOT yourself up in regret by not trying again and again. When asked about his 10,000 failed attempts, Thomas Edison, the inventor of the lightbulb, said, "I have not failed, I've just found 10,000 ways that won't work." Ten thousand times and two times is a huge difference. Try it again.

A Carpenter's Story

I read a story from an unknown author about a carpenter who was ready to retire. He told his employer-contractor of his plans to leave the house-building business and live a more leisurely life with his wife enjoying his extended family. He would miss the paycheck, but he needed to retire. They could get by.

The contractor was sorry to see his good worker go and asked if he could build just one more house as a personal favor. The carpenter said yes, but his heart was not in his work anymore. He resorted to shoddy workmanship and used inferior materials. It was an unfortunate way to end his career.

When the carpenter finished his work and the builder came to inspect the house, the contractor handed the front-door key to the carpenter. "This is your house," he said, "my gift to you."

 Short-timers disease is a killer.

What a shock! What a missed gift! If he had only known he was building his own house, he would have done it all so differently. He got the dreaded case of short-timers disease, which is typically at the cost of the employer who continues paying someone who quits but stays! This carpenter was the one who really paid the price. Now he had to live in the home he had carelessly built.

So it is with us. We build our lives in a distracted way, reacting rather than acting, willing to put up with less than the best. At important points, we do not give the job our best effort. Then, with a shock, we look at the situation we have created and find that we are now living in the house we have built. If we had realized that, we would have done it differently.

Perhaps think of yourself in this story. Think about this house as your life. Each day, you hammer a nail, place a board, or erect a wall. Build wisely. It is the only life you will ever build. Even if you live it for only one day more, that day deserves to be truly lived.

If we want to build a regret-proof life, this is a really good story to remember. Build it sturdy, build it with the best tools you can afford. Don't be embarrassed about how beautiful and full your house turns out. That's how this game of life is played.

CHAPTER 6

SIZE MATTERS: BE EMBARRASSED

*"It's not the size of the dog in the fight,
It's the size of the fight in the dog."*

—MARK TWAIN

That Mark Twain quote is probably where the modern day "GO BIG or GO HOME" quote originated. Too many people forget the GO BIG part and just remember GO HOME!

I'll confess my big embarrassing dream is to lead MILLIONS to discover their WHY, or some call it their purpose.

I love GO-BIG stories! One of my favorites is the awesome friendship story about a Saudi Arabian prince and an American golf pro who became almost immediate best friends during the Prince's two-week golf trip to the U.S.

After the two weeks of golfing, while the two exchanged farewells, the Saudi prince invited the American pro to Saudi for a golf vacation. The prince even offered to pick the pro up in his private jet. The pro accepted, went, and had an equally wonderful time. Upon departing the royal plane, the prince said he wanted to give the pro a gift for coming to his country to golf and asked what kinds of things the pro liked. The pro said, "Are you kidding me?" reminding the prince that he just stayed in a palace for two weeks after being personally flown over and back on a private jet, golfing on the best courses in his country, ultimately suggesting he had already received the best gift ever. But the prince insisted explaining it was customary in his culture to give a gift as a token of appreciation. The pro finally agreed, sharing with the prince that he collected golf clubs.

For the next several weeks, the pro watched for a delivery. He secretly wondered if it would be gold-plated and how the monogram would look. He knew it would be super nice. But week after week, no club arrived.

Finally, one day, he received a certified letter in a normal-sized envelope. He was super disappointed but not for long because in that envelope was the deed to a 500-acre golf course! Yeah, you read that right. Not a golf-club, but a golf course!

Size Matters: Be Embarrassed

This pro was thinking small—he wasn't thinking royalty-sized anything. That concept was too big for him! Where would you have fallen in this story?

I tell you that story because the same thing happens with our purpose, our why, our dream (whatever you want to call it). So many of us are too scared or proud to go big with our dreams and aspirations—at least out loud. My rule of thumb is your dream should be so big you're embarrassed to say it out loud.

Yes, let embarrassment be your measuring stick!

I am blessed to have parents who never set boundaries on what my siblings or I could dream or achieve. They never said, "You can't go to college, you can't move away, you can't be the president." No, they did just the opposite and told us we had the capacity for anything! Any kNOTS set on my life were tied by the unholy trinity... me, myself and I!

> *"Some people dream of great accomplishments, while others stay awake and do them."*
>
> —UNKNOWN

Go ahead and start dreaming big embarrassing dreams! Then take action. Let's start with the very first step together. Maybe your dream isn't listed, so fill yours in.

BLUE SKY DREAMING STARTS HERE
I DREAM ABOUT HAVING
I DREAM ABOUT BECOMING
I DREAM ABOUT HELPING
I DREAM ABOUT FIXING
I DREAM ABOUT INVENTING
I DREAM ABOUT SAVING
I DREAM ABOUT ERADICATING
I DREAM ABOUT SPEAKING
I DREAM ABOUT WRITING
I DREAM ABOUT GOING TO
IF I HAD ALL THE MONEY IN THE WORLD, I WOULD
I DREAM ABOUT

Now, transfer it to a Post-it note or note card and tape it up in multiple locations at home and work! Let everyone see it! Get them used to seeing what is in store for the world. I had **_UNTIE EVERY kNOT_** taped on my bathroom mirror for over a YEAR! I had to move around it to different places on the same mirror multiple times because it would become invisible. I finally took it down when I sent the book to my editorial board. I should have taken a picture of it to show you how gnarly it got.

On my desk, I have a Louis L' Amour quote: *"Start writing, no matter what. The water does not flow until the faucet is turned on."*

CHAPTER 7

Rejection-Proof Yourself

*Even a turtle doesn't get ahead
unless he sticks his neck out!*

I guarantee you 1,000 percent that in our lives, we will reject ourselves more times than all the other people combined. So tell me again, why are we so afraid of rejection? Do you think God ever gets sad and asks, *"What do you mean you're rejecting yourself? I worked so hard on you!"*

Rejection comes in all shapes and sizes, both personal and professional, by loved ones and friends and trusted colleagues alike. Often, because we're hurt, we inflate a situation and call it rejection when it wasn't meant to be rejection. Then, other times, we turn objection into rejection. How we handle rejection is a choice. Our choice. I'll tell you about one of my million personal stories later in the chapter.

When I speak to audiences, I remind them that rejection and objection are not the same. For example, when we receive pushback to what we're saying, suggesting, or selling, that is just an objection. That is someone saying they're not interested in the "what" we're saying, suggesting or selling. We need to be super careful not to play a mind game with ourselves and convert objection into personal rejection. The two are very different.

Let's take this book for an example. I'm often asked by people how they can share the information in this book with someone who could really benefit from it, but will reject it because they don't believe they need it or will benefit from it? My answer is prayerful preparation. Prepare your delivery. I always say, where God guides, He provides. Another is, do your best, and He will do the rest! Before you offer unsolicited advice or recommendations, prepare for potential responses to rejection-proof yourself.

Our company implements and manages sales programs in hospitals and health systems across the country. Therefore, we conduct a ton of sales training and training programs. In my opinion, preparation is the secret sauce to great sales results. It forces you to do your homework on the subject and prepare for all the likely or unlikely reactions you might receive. It's equivalent to great test taking: The more prepared you are, the easier the test seems and the better your results.

We like the P^6 Principle: Proper prior preparation prevents poor performance. Regardless of what is being sold, including a concept or idea, a service or product—it's sales. As Zig Ziglar said, "We are all in the sales, but only the brave ones admit it." Anyone ever tried to sell a kid on eating their vegetables or doing their homework? How about selling your spouse on why you need to buy x, y, or z? Get my point? We're all in sales—even YOU!

Now that I've "sold you" on the reality that we're all in sales, let me complete the sale on the value of preparation and tell you about when even this teacher fell short and faced rejection. I mean seriously, I teach it, I preach it; I eat, sleep, and breathe preparation... until I didn't.

I made a monumental mistake with one of my hospital clients in front of the entire executive team, including the hospital's CEO, COO, CFO, CMO, CNO CSO, etc. Those are all acronyms for a Chief of something. The top brass of a hospital or health system. They had been my client for a couple years, and I had grown comfortable being transparent. The CEO was a no nonsense leader who was painfully honest and upfront. The Chief Medical Officer was borderline crude with his frankness.

The purpose of my attendance at the Chiefs' meeting was to provide an update on market share growth that had occurred, in large part due to the collective efforts of the Outreach (sales) program. Sadly, the growth results could have been even better with better internal collaboration. Stay with me, it's about to get juicy.

I spent considerable time preparing for the meeting. I had a PowerPoint presentation showing data with colorful charts and graphs. I was on top of it. They had a wildly successful growth year, and the story was great. Despite this team of Chiefs not always playing well together, we had a success story. I even purchased and brought a celebratory gift for each of them.

The data presentation went great, and I finished answering their questions and thanked them for their support. Then I presented the celebratory gift. As I distributed the gift, the bottom quickly fell out from underneath me.

The gift was a great book and companion workbook by the best-selling author and speaker Patrick Lencioni. The book provided real-life successful team stories about challenges, opportunities, and creative solutions. As I distributed the book and workbook, I shared that one of our other hospital client's entire executive team was currently using it as a leadership book club. I didn't love the book's title, but I loved the abundance of valuable real-life information it contained. The title was *The Five Dysfunctions of a Team.*

Friends, as I handed it out, the tension in the room became so obvious so quickly that you would have thought I just told them they all were infected with the plague and would die soon. It was the title, I thought, so I made a few jokes about the title to attempt to remove the tension. They believed I was calling them dysfunctional.

They are awesome people, and like most teams that want to remain relevant and effective, there are areas that could be improved. In fact, I personally witnessed this team competing, back-biting, and fighting like siblings, so much so that the CEO had to intervene more than once. Regardless, I was an outsider who clearly hit a cord!

While one "C" member spoke up nervously, admitting they could really use this book, the others remained completely silent. Some wouldn't even make eye contact with me. I felt completely rejected and finally understood the old saying, "No good deed goes unpunished."

It got worse. Later that day, I was secretly copied on an email the CEO sent to that entire executive team asking if anyone else was bothered by my gift. I wanted to scream "**IT'S A BOOK, PEOPLE!**" But wait, there's more! Less than a week later, I received a package from the Chief Medical Officer. In the package was "the book" with a small note card that read, "NO THANKS, Dr. H." I still have that card pinned to my board so I can remember what mean-ignorance looks and feels like.

So, what went wrong? Several things! First, I gave a gift to a team that was in desperate need of the information, but they were in complete denial... at least publicly. It was easier to criticize or reject it than it was to have an open mind to research-based information.

Second, I thought I had earned the trusted-advisor status with them and that they would love to have research-based evidence on how to take their team to another level, not to mention take their growth results to another level, which was what they hired me to do.

And third, the one I know best, my lack of preparation. I went for the "other clients are using it" line, but I neglected to prepare by playing the "what if" game. What if they are offended?

Sadly, our relationship was never the same.

Sometimes our best intentions and well-meaning gifts will be rejected. I said the "best intentions and well-meaning gifts" will be rejected, not us personally. They rejected the book and the need for improvement. While I was extremely bothered that I offended them, I made a conscious decision not to stamp myself as rejected. That is how we become rejection-proof, by not allowing the rejection kNOT to hold us back.

Why are we so afraid of rejection? Just the thought of rejection can tie a huge kNOT around us. I truly believe the fear of regret is just our stupid pride. What do you have to lose but your pride? Most people are so proud that they literally fear rejection more than they fear missing out on an opportunity to help someone or fulfill their dreams. You're less likely to fear rejection if you reframe where the rejection is pointed.

 There will always be someone who can't see your worth. Just don't let it be YOU.

Just like every kNOT, rejection is a choice. Knowing that you literally have a super-power called choice can not only set you free but can also make you rejection-proof. Remember, the more successful you are or get at something, the more the critics will surface. That is when I always remember the quote from Zig Ziglar:

"Don't be distracted by criticism. Remember the only taste of success some people have is when they take a bite out of you."

–Zig Ziglar

CHAPTER 8

YOU WERE MADE FOR MORE

Make no mistake, God will accomplish ALL He wants to accomplish. The question is, will you let Him do it through YOU?

How many people does it take to make a difference? ONE! There has never been nor will there ever be another YOU! Think about that. You're a one of a kind. You will always win a first-place gold medal in being you! No one else can ever beat you. That miracle is in your hands. You possess something only you can give to the world. What's it going to be, friend?

You remember the story of Adam and Eve in the Garden of Eden? Remember when they ate the apple from the tree that God told them not to, and suddenly, their eyes were open to their nakedness? Then when God showed up, they hid from Him. God asked, "Where are you?"

Now we know God knew exactly where they were and what they had done. That is the same for us. God knows where we are and what we've done. I believe He is asking the same question to each of us. Where are you?

I want to talk to you about something that is near and dear to my heart: Your purpose. I believe my purpose is to lead millions of people to discover their purpose, sometimes called their WHY. Some of you already know your purpose, and I celebrate you! In my travels and published research, the vast majority of people across all genders, ages, and socioeconomic groups don't feel they know their purpose or what they were made for.

My goal is to convince you that you were made for more than you can imagine! Notice that earlier, I used the words YOUR purpose and YOUR why. *Not your* kids' why, your spouse's why, your boss' why, your parent's why... NOPE. I want to talk about what you were made for—your why—your purpose.

Your Purpose

This subject has puzzled people for centuries.

A Northwestern University philosophy professor wrote to 250 of the best-known philosophers, scientists, writers, and intellectuals across the world, asking them, "What is the meaning of life?" He then published their responses in a book.

Some offered their best guesses. Some admitted that they just made up a purpose for life. Others were honest enough to say they were clueless! Funny though, several asked him to write back and tell them what he discovered as the purpose of life.

USA Today conducted a poll asking people, "If you could ask God one question, what would it be?" By far, the number one answer was, "What is my purpose?"

For those who don't know, you're in good company because this question has puzzled people since the beginning of time.

Mark Twain said that the two most important days in your life are the day you were born and the day you discover why.

Tale of Two Tribes

There's an old tale about two enemy tribes. One tribe settled on the top of the mountain, the other in the valley. Neither tribe bothered the other until one day, the highlander tribe brutally attacked the lowlanders. They burned most of the village, robbed them, and even kidnapped a baby. After the initial shock had passed and they assessed the damage, the leaders of the tribe promised the mother that they would put a group of warriors together to rescue her child.

The warriors set out up the mountain on the rescue mission. About halfway up a very rough terrain, unable to find tracks or paths to the top, they contemplated abandoning the mission and returning to camp. At that time, they saw a speck heading down the mountain in their direction. They didn't know if it was an animal or a man. The object got closer and closer until they realized it was a woman. Not just any woman but the mother of the kidnapped baby. On her back was the rescued baby.

They were in shock and just asked, "how?" They reminded her that they were strong warriors and had struggled to climb the rough terrain. She just gave a four-word answer: "**It's not your baby!**"

Until you understand YOUR purpose is YOUR baby, you won't OWN IT, and you are at risk of missing out. The problem is you're not the only person who will miss out. Candidly, the world misses out!

 Is has to be your baby!

YOUR PURPOSE: 4 WAYS TO HELP UNCOVER WHAT YOU WERE MADE FOR

#1: Be the One

There are three types of people: quitters, campers, and climbers. Select the category into which you fall.

QUITTERS: The quitters are often bitter, resentful, and the loudest whiners. BOO-HOO! They retired 20 years ago but never told anyone. Did you know that the two most common times people quit are after defeat and after victory? The ironic thing is successful people fail more than average people.

It's always better to fail in doing something than to excel in doing nothing. There is a funny 50/90 saying, "They died when they were 50, but we didn't bury them until they were 90!" I think that's where the term "walking dead" came from.

CAMPERS: The campers work hard to find a safe plateau in life. They would say that they have been aiming for this spot all their lives, and now, they can finally camp. The good news is that inside every camper is a climber. If you're alive, you still have more climbing to do!

CLIMBERS: The climbers never stop learning and growing. Climbers are relentless in their pursuit of their lifetime goals and purpose. They inspire others to see their full potential. They know it's not just about them! They have purpose and passion in what they do regardless of their age, job, or spot in life.

Did you find yourself in any of the categories? Now what is your plan?

If you've never heard of or read much about a Prophet named Jeremiah, you might consider it because his story is so relevant today! God used Jeremiah (who was super young) to warn people of the price they would pay if they didn't clean up their act. By people, I mean an entire county.

Jeremiah was super scared and reminded God how young he was (as if God didn't know). God told Jeremiah to look for just one [obedient] person among all the disobedient and He would cancel the pending destruction... JUST ONE!

It's like watching an intense movie, I want to scream, "Wake up dumb-dumb! What's your problem? GET UP! Can't you see what's in store for you?" But aren't we the very same way? It's so easy to see what others should do and exclude ourselves.

God looked for just one person! **Be the one!** Be the one person who ignites the fire in your family, your workplace, and your world! You have been chosen; the rest is up to you!

 Be the one!

#2: Be In The Moment: Where The Magic Happens

As long as I remember, this is where I've struggled and tied some of my biggest kNOTS. See if you find yourself on this team.

I'm either focused on what's next: the next event, project, day, meal—the next *anything*—or I'm focused on the past with "shoulda-coulda-woulda" disorder! Basically, I focus on any time but NOW, and this is why I wrote the later chapter entitled "Now Is the Time."

I struggle with this even though, I'm sure just like you, I totally understand we only have right now. The past is over, and we're not guaranteed the future. You know a not-so-fun fact: Death can show up any time, and it does not call ahead or make reservations.

There is this thing called DESTRUCTION BY DISTRACTION. It is difficult to detect when it's happening because it doesn't involve bad things but good things that take the place of the most important things. When we allow ourselves to be lured into believing the trivial and spend our life focused on the unimportant, it keeps us from our calling and deprived of our destiny!

Today, it's a bigger challenge with a communication device always in our hand. Sometimes, weapons are disguised as tools! What are YOUR weapons of mass DISTRACTION?

#3: Be Intentional

What if your purpose is to set someone or something historical into motion?

It doesn't matter if you're 16 or 96—God has given you unique abilities, talents and gifts. They were pre-designed just for you! There's one popular bible verse where God said, "Before I formed in the womb, I knew you. Before you were born, I set you apart" (Jeremiah 1:5).

But we get so busy living our lives and going through the motions without being intentional that life just flies by—and we miss it! It's a *use it or lose it* deal. Many of us suffer from "Someday Syndrome."

Time has an equal opportunity guarantee. We all get 24 hours. It doesn't matter who you are. Rich, poor, famous, or unknown—we all get the same amount each day. What do the most successful people in the world have in common? They all have the exact same 24 hours each day, but *perhaps they used their time differently.*

 Many of us suffer from Someday Syndrome!

We can make more money, we can buy more stuff, we can eat, drink, and be merry. We can tear up our bodies, we can get fat and then have it sucked, tucked, and lifted. But we—YOU—can't get more time!

ARE YOU A SLEEPWALKER?

A friend of mine said something that really resonated with me. She experienced a bad break-up and said she went into survival mode and stayed there. She called it sleep-walking, saying, *"I was sleep-walking through life."*

Hearing that was a major AH-HA moment for me. It's a great description of why many of us are missing our real purpose as we go through the motions of life. The thing about motion is it doesn't have one speed or even speed limits. Maybe for some of us, we're sleep-running, even sprinting through life. What about you?

 I was sleepwalking through life.

We give "being intentional" such lip service—until given a death sentence—then it's a painful reality! Are you being intentional with your life?

#4: Expose Yourself (And Others)

By exposing, I don't mean something like open your trench coach flasher, neither do I mean ratting yourself or someone out. What I mean by exposing yourself is that we often don't give exposure or are exposed to more or different things because we just don't know what we don't know. That is why we must be intentional about <u>exposing ourselves</u>—and the people in our lives—to more, to different, to the unknown!

We're limited (or imprinted) by our environment, by what we know or what our parents/teachers/friends know PERIOD & END OF STORY. I had this revelation, and as a mother, it filled me with Catholic guilt (I'm not even a Catholic anymore), even though it was innocent ignorance.

Do you ever notice that families seem to have a lot of the same occupations? If there is an educator, you see a lot of teachers. Doctors breed doctors. Lawyers have more lawyers than non-lawyer families. College-educated parents typically force their kids to attend college. Sadly, there is also a bad side of that principle too. You can probably recall some not-so-good examples too. Why is that? Because we are imprinted based on our environment. We model or learn from what we see.

I'm in the business side of healthcare, so guess what? Both of my kids are in healthcare. That is what they saw growing up. So, what's the problem? The problem is healthcare is all I exposed them to. It was what I knew, so I exposed them to all things healthcare. Our family entertainment was water sports. Today, both kids would and have lived on the water. What was my life, became theirs too.

So the problem really is, if we don't know how to expose ourselves to new things, how on earth can we help, teach or model the way for others?

On commercial flights, the flight attendants always get on the intercom system and give the life and death safety instructions. If you recall, part of the safety instructions include:

If the cabin pressure changes, oxygen masks will fall from the ceiling. To start the flow of oxygen, pull the mask toward you. Place it firmly over your nose and mouth, secure the elastic band behind your head, and breathe normally. If you are travelling with a child or (someone who acts like a child) who needs assistance, secure your mask first and then assist the other person.

We confuse focusing on ourselves as selfish! Perhaps it's really one of our kNOTS. We can't help others when we're messed up. Expose yourself first, then expose others!

CHAPTER 9

Excuses, Excuses: Burn Your Bucket

If you're serious about untying your kNOTS, you'll find a way; if you're not, you'll find an excuse.

This is my tough-love chapter. If that made you want to fast-forward to the next chapter, DON'T! That's probably a sign there is a golden nugget waiting right here for you.

A man dies and goes to heaven. He meets St. Peter at the Pearly Gates where St. Peter proceeds with a customary tour. As they're walking down the streets of gold, they pass a big warehouse. St. Peter doesn't mention anything, but the guy noticed the door is cracked and peeks inside. He noticed gift boxes beautifully wrapped and stacked as high and far as his eyes can see. He asks Peter about the warehouse, but Peter blows him off, saying this is where all the gifts are stored. The man asked if he had one. Peter replied, yes, everyone has a gift. The man asked to see his gift, so they searched through the warehouse to find it. When the man opened his gift, it said World's Most Famous Astronaut.

The man looked at Peter perplexed and said, "Wait, I always wanted to be an astronaut." Peter said, "I know." The guy said, "When I was a child, I dreamed of becoming an astronaut. My parents bought me a telescope, and I would spend hours looking up at the stars and planets." Peter said, "I know." Guy said, "But I, uh, got older and got distracted with friends and playing." Peter said, "I know." "But then I took a bunch of science classes in high school and even in college, but I..." Peter said, "I know."

Do you see where this story is going? The guy always felt that was his gift, but chose not to open and use it.

What does your gift box hold? When you're standing at the gates and St. Peter takes you for the tour, will your box have no surprises in it? Will the ribbon already be untied?

 What does your gift box hold?

God gave us all a gift or gifts. I love talking about gifts and talents because I'm reminded that **YOU CAN'T RECEIVE A GIFT WITHOUT A GIFT-GIVER.** But we must choose to open the gift and activate the plan. Our purpose.

Did you hear a lot of buts in that story? Buts are EXCUSES! Buts are kNOTS! Do you have a but that is holding you back? We must get our buts out of the way.

DESTINY DELAYED IS THE DEVIL'S DELIGHT

The devil wants to steal your power and neutralize your impact. His goal is to trick you with the trivial and get you to spend your life focused on anything else, any excuse to keep you from your calling and depriving you of your destiny.

Most people think they don't have any power for the devil to steal. Well, there's a favorite neutralizing lie straight from the devil. Stay in bed and don't work out today. There's another trivial but real lie from the devil keeping you from being your best and healthiest self!

If you're good at making excuses, it will be difficult to be great at anything else. Excuses will always be there for you, but opportunities won't.

In the 60's there was a burn-your-bra feminist movement. I laugh because there isn't a woman on this planet who needs a movement for that! I want to start a burn-your-bucket movement—your excuse bucket, that is! If you tracked the number of excuses you make a day, I wonder how many that would be.

Excuses are about just bouts with doubt! We all have doubts, but let's not turn them into kNOTs.

Christopher Reeves, better known as Superman, used to say, *"So many of our dreams at first seem impossible, then they seem improbable, and then, when we summon the will, they become the inevitable."*

We have a tendency to over complicate the simplest things in life. I love what the late Jack Welch, Former CEO of General Electric, used to say. He said. *"You can't believe how hard it is for people to be simple, how much they fear being simple. They worry that if they're simple, people will think they're simpleminded. In reality, of course, it's just the reverse."*

IT'S TAKING TOO LONG EXCUSE

It took Noah 120 years to build the ark, but Noah didn't complain or make excuses. Listen, the man had NEVER seen rain—that takes faith. God didn't say, "Build any kind of boat." (And in reality, it was more like a ship than a boat.) He was very specific. I think the same applies to our gifts. Noah trusted God completely, and that made God smile. That needs to be a goal for all of us... make God smile!

I DON'T FEEL COMFORTABLE EXCUSE

Your comfort zone is a beautiful thing, but you will never grow there. Remember, coming into your calling means coming out of your comfort zone. No one ever reaches their potential in their comfort zone. Maybe your comfort zone is binge-watching a great Netflix series. It is mine! But books don't get written in front of the television. I know that for a fact!

Maybe your comfort zone is fitting in. The fact is, most of us grew up working hard to fit in. Although, in today's busy world, we're told the only way to experience real success is to be different, to stand out from all the rest! So which is it?

In his book *Purple Cow: Transform Your Business by Being Remarkable*, Seth Godin promotes just that, the importance of standing out. It makes sense! The real question is why and how did we ever buy-in to the fitting-in, copycat rule?

So many of the incredible people in my life, past and present, are the ones who are different, who stand out from the crowd in many wonderful and different ways. I'm not saying they're louder, brighter, or smarter. I'm saying they're true to themselves and their gifts that make them different, and being different "makes *the* difference!"

What do you think is better: fitting in or standing out? Is it possible to stand out in a GREAT way, while fitting in, so that we don't alienate the people or business we're trying to attract? How can we stand out *and* fit in?

So, the next time you're trying to fit in, give the world a gift and just be YOU. We all stink at trying to be someone else. We are the world's experts at being ourselves. When you really stay true to your own purple-and-pink polka dot, black, white, or green unique **YOU**, you have all the ingredients to stand out... and fit it... but mostly to be the perfect *same difference!*

Why do we so easily default to excuses, anyway? Here is the reason—see if you can guess who this is.

I am your constant companion. I am your greatest helper or heaviest burden. I will push you onward or drag you down to failure. I am completely at your command. Half of the things you do you might as well turn over to me, and I will do them quickly and correctly. I am easily managed; you must be firm with me. Show me exactly how you want something done, and after a few lessons, I will do it automatically. I am the servant of great people, and alas, of all failures as well. Those who are great, I have made great. Those who are failures, I have made failures. I am not a machine, though I work with the precision of a machine plus the intelligence of a person. You may run me for profit or run me for ruin; it makes no difference to me. Take me, train me, be firm with me, and I will place the world at your feet. Be easy with me, and I will destroy you. **WHO AM I?**

Did you guess "conscience"? Many people do. The answer is HABIT. Making excuses easily becomes a habit.

We may not be able to decide our future, but we absolutely, positively decide our habits, and then our habits decide our futures. Most of our habits start in our head, justifying our kNOTS. Make a habit of talking to yourself like you would to someone you love. The infamous Henry Ford said, "Whether you think you can, or think you can't, either way, you're right."

What excuse are you using that's holding you back from fulfilling your purpose? I've used almost all of them. I'm not going to lie and say breaking a habit isn't hard work. Look in the mirror: That's your competition.

Do you tell yourself, I'm too old or too young? Is your go-to, I don't have the looks, the hair, skin or body? Or perhaps you get much more specific. I'm too fat, too saggy or flabby. I'm too short, I'm too tall, I'm too thin (well, I've used two of those). I have too many wrinkles or stretch marks... Friends, those are battle scars, souvenirs from your main events, like babies, good food, laughing and living!

Perhaps you struggle with an addiction or illness that's now become your kNOT. Turn your mess into a message and step into your destiny!

It's kNOT my fault! Oh all the blame-game excuses are so powerful. Excuses like *my parents didn't push me* or some use, *my parents pushed me too hard!* It's his/her fault, he/she walked out on me! It's "their" fault, whoever the heck "THEY" are!

How about, I'm still upset about [fill in the blank]. Friend, that excuse is called a GRUDGE, which you are carrying around. And hear me now, *you can't walk into your future if you're still hanging on to your past!* Holding a grudge is like drinking poison and expecting someone else to get sick.

If we're not picking on our bodies or blaming others, sadly, there is another laundry list of other excuses.

I don't have the right education. I don't make enough money. I have a day job that sucks. Like many successful people, you may have to work your day job on your way to your dream job.

Maybe your go-to is, "I don't have time." Just know that kNOT is generally a lack of direction, not lack of time. We all have 24-hour days.

How about, "I don't know what I'm supposed to do!" Let me rip off the Band-Aid and be the one to tell you that *it ain't gonna fall out of the sky.* So, get up, dress up, and show up to your life!

"I'm scared" is a huge kNOT of an excuse. Perhaps it's related to discovering your purpose or just taking the first step at trying something new. Try turning your fear into excitement. If that sounds weird, think about how scary but exhilarating going to a haunted house, escape room, OR roller coaster ride is. Anything worth doing is often scary. Don't use it as an excuse—perhaps use it as your horsepower.

What excuse is holding you back from the BIG purpose you were born to live? The real question is, *are you open to recognizing your excuse from what's real?*

You know the cliché "the devil is in the details"? The devil is almost always in the detail of excuses! If the devil can keep you so busy, keeping your attention diverted until you're dead, he will be able to get you to do to yourself what he does not have the power to do to you. Remember, the devil comes only to steal, kill, and destroy—that's it! His end game is to play the fiddle while the life <u>you were meant to live</u> goes up in smoke!

Excuses for Dear Younger Me

As it relates to excuses, what would you tell your younger self instead of using one of the excuses mentioned above?

Go to that class reunion, wedding, or funeral. As it relates to a funeral, just a quick public service announcement: GO! Don't use excuses like "I haven't seen them in years" or "the family won't know me." I spoke to a mother who lost her son, and she said she was SO GRATEFUL TO SEE EVERYONE! She said now that she understands the joy even strangers who knew her son brought, she would never ever use an excuse or hesitate to attend a funeral again.

What would you tell yourself to **GO FOR**, to do? Go for that dream, that job, that relationship, that TRIP! Go learn that language, that instrument, that subject.

If you're still breathing, it's not too late to do or don't do! If you're thinking, "No, that person is gone, that job is gone, or that train has left the station," let me be crystal clear: It wasn't your person, it wasn't your job, and it wasn't your train!

The fact is, we can't change the past, but we can learn from it, and we can control a lot of our future.

Quit making excuses, and quit waiting for the right time. If it's not important, you'll make excuses. When it is important, you'll make it happen.

CHAPTER 10

You Go First, but Don't Be Weird

It's kNOT what you have—it's what you do with what you have.

It sounds simple, until it's your turn to go first. Then it's not. There's a delicate line between being the first and being the weird one.

When I say weird, I mean being over-zealous about something that turns people off or away. We want to model the way by being innovative and brave. But too, often our excitement gets out of balance. Research shows we have such little time to make a first impression—we never want to create a kNOT between us and someone who we're trying to impact.

Speaking of first, did you know psychologists at Princeton University suggest that first impressions are made in as short as one-tenth of a second? Snap your finger, and that was longer than one tenth of one second. Sadly, often before we have time to open our mouths, people have formed an impression. How the heck can we make an impact when we only have a one-tenth of a second to make a first impression?

Oftentimes, it's that eye contact, or they hear what you're saying before they see you. Or the speed of your approach. Are you so excited that you scare them? When people look at you, what qualities do they see on display?

Have you ever noticed how some people get ahold of something new and they get so obsessed about it that they turn weird and you avoid them like the plague? They've started selling a new revolutionary product, but they get so wildly enthusiastic, you can barely handle five minutes with them. I'm cracking up just thinking about the things I've seen and done! It's really just about excitement, but sometimes, we get so "on fire" for the new thing that we have a difficult time containing it and quickly cross over to the weird team.

Don't get me wrong—I like weird... Have you met me? I like weird in the sense that you're being your genuine self, discovering your purpose and dancing to the beat of your own drum. I don't consider it weird when we're not being a follower of the "in crowd." When

I say weird, team, I'm talking about becoming uncomfortable to be around... Does make sense? Who on this earth will we impact if people are uncomfortable being around us? Absolutely no one!

I've seen it with people who just start selling a product, be it make-up, jewelry, life insurance. I LOVE entrepreneurship; that is what our country is all about. We just have to know how to be enthusiastic and believe in what we're promoting but stay on the non-weird side.

I've also seen it in the church when someone first discovers who Jesus is and what He did for them, and they get so excited, they turn weird—and then wonder why people are turned off by the church.

I specifically want to talk about this last one. If you're not a follower of Jesus, you actually have a greater radar, if you will, at identifying these kinds of weirdos in the crowd. In the '70s, they called these people Jesus freaks. I've heard lots of terms, like tent churches, Kool-Aid drinkers, etc. Sadly, I believe the main reason people are turned off or uncomfortable talking about Jesus is because we've made it weird by acting weird.

I am a Christian. That means I believe in Jesus and that He came to earth to carry our sins to hell so when we die, we go to heaven. He did it for me and you too. In fact, neither you nor I have ever locked eyes with someone God does not love. I try to not be weird but also not lukewarm about Jesus—because that is a major offense to God.

My husband was a Christian long before I was, but he was never weird. Different yes, but in a mysterious and good way. Don't get me wrong, he is a manly man in every way (wink wink). But instead of preaching, he modeled such a lifestyle that drew people to him. He taught me that the best way to introduce a non-believer in Jesus is through our life, through our actions. Now I too want to live in such a way that those who know me but don't know Jesus, will want to know Jesus because they know me. I love how the Apostle Paul asked, *How can people believe in Jesus if they've never heard about Him? And how can they hear about Him unless someone tells them?*

Fact is, some people will only hear about Jesus through our actions! They believe they learn far more by our actions than by our words. I remember reading a question that stopped me in my tracks: Is anyone going to be in heaven because of you? Right now can literally count forever.

 When God says it's "SHOWTIME," there's not a single person who can say "CUT."

BE THE ONE

I heard a story once about a forest fire that erupted. The forest was super quiet, and from out of nowhere came sounds of animals running by, then quiet again. Shortly after, flames ignited the dry forest. "Fire!" roared the one animal. "Run for your lives!" cried another. The forest animals, great and small, ran for their lives.

One small concerned bird asked what they could do. No other animal answered—they all just ran. So he flew to the water and grabbed a bill-full of water and flew back and forth dropping bill-fulls of water onto the fire.

High above, angels were watching this unfold. One angel asked the others what that bird was doing. The other said he was trying to put the fire out one bill-full at a time. "But why?" The angel asked. They couldn't figure out what was happening, so one angel was sent to find out.

Later, the angel returned, surrounded by the other angels anxiously awaiting an answer. "Well?" they asked, "What is he doing?"

The angel replied softly, "He told me, 'I am only one, and I cannot do everything, but I can do something.'" The angels were all so touched they all started to cry, and their tears created a rain shower that fell on the flames below, drowning out the fire. Moral of the story: Do what you can with what you've been given. Be the one!

UNDERSTANDING WHO YOU ARE

I want to share a story about a chicken and an eagle.[3] I want you to become a chicken in your mind. I want you to imagine that you are the star of my chicken story.

You're really an eagle, but you're being raised in a chicken coop. Your peers, who model the way for you, are chickens, *good chickens*, but they too were raised in the coop.

You've learned to bawk like a chicken, dig like a chicken, make a hole and get down in it on a hot summer day. You've learned to cluck when another chicken lays an egg. You have become a really good chicken!

You have been *"imprinted,"* a term that psychologists use when you *behave* according to your environment.

But... you're really a very beautiful eagle *out in this chicken yard*. One day, along comes a male eagle flying over the chicken coop, and he sees the female eagle down there doing all these chicken things! He circles because he cannot believe what he sees. He hovers a little too long so his shadow falls on the coop, and one of the chickens lets out a bawk. They all run into the chicken house because it was an eagle—a predator.

So the eagle hides up in a tree and watches the chicken coop for days, until one day the female eagle wanders just far enough away from the coop that he's certain he can intercept her before she could get back, so he swoops down and cuts her off while all the other chickens get into the chicken house.

He has her cornered, and all the other chickens were inside clucking.

Well, she said, if that's true, then you'll get out of my way and won't block me if I wanted to leave... will you?

NO! he said. Look, I'll step over here... and as he steps aside, she runs right back to her comfort zone: the chicken house. Safely inside the chicken house, she tells all her chicken friends how she outsmarted the eagle. They all clapped, shouting, Wow, great job, Chicken Little!

Now STOP!

If you think about that story for a minute, can you find yourself in any of it? Do you have a comfort zone—a chicken coop that you gravitate to—knowing full well you don't belong there?

Have you ever been knocked down after you've mustered up the courage to tell a chicken who you are and your plans to soar, and they've laughed because they think you're kidding or respond with, Who do you think you are? I have!

I shared with someone very dear to me that I was going to lead millions to discover their purpose. You know, my embarrassing-sized dream? That person bawked like a chicken, I kid you not! This person is wonderful but is stuck on me remaining focused on my day job—running the company. It felt like they wanted me to stay in the coop. But just like you, I know God has a bigger vision. In fact, one of my favorite Bible verses confirms it: *No eye has seen, no ear has heard, no mind can conceive the wonderful things God has in store for those who love Him.* Can you imagine, it's so big our minds can't even conceive it? I do have the opportunity and use my day job platform in leading millions to discover their purpose. My title for many years was Chief Motivational Officer for a reason! How can you use your current platform? There is no impact without contact! Remember, life is a contact sport.

 There is always someone who can't see your worth—
JUST DON'T LET IT BE YOU!

Even though that didn't stop me, it did hurt me deeply. But I chose to turn that hurt into fuel! We cannot hold a GRUDGE because, as I said before, it will just poison us.

You may work around a bunch of chickens. You may live with chickens or have relatives that still think they're chickens. But we must draw that line in the sand and say, "I may be in a limited environment, but I am not settling here because I AM AN EAGLE!"

Let's get something clear right here, right now, today! Some of you have been in that chicken coop way too long. Let me tell you what you already know: You're not a chicken. YOU ARE AN EAGLE!

Don't let a limited environment rub off on you. Don't let how you were raised, or what someone said, keep you from knowing who you really are.

As a woman of faith, I believe all we need to do is check out our spiritual birth certificate. There, we will find we've been made in the image of almighty God. He crowned us with favor. We have royal blood flowing through our veins. We are not just eagles—we are royal eagles! You were **never** created to be average or mediocre. YOU WERE MADE FOR MORE!

CHAPTER 11
SHOW ME YOUR FRIENDS

*Show me your friends,
and I'll show you your future.*

Growing up, my mom would always say, "You are who you hang with, Tammy." When my kids were growing up, I better understood what she meant. I could tell who my kids had spent time with based on their behavior or attitude when they came home. In the event they were not so pleasant, I would literally hug them and tell them that I was squeezing the ugly out. It actually works; try it with your kids. I'll never forget when I was crabby and complaining about something and my daughter turned the table and came up and hugged me. She whispered in my ear, "I'm squeezing the ugly out of you!" It is particularly powerful when your children use your tricks on you! It is true, the apple doesn't fall far from the tree.

Quick story about a king recorded in history to be one of the wisest and richest men ever. His name was Solomon, and his extravagant reign was worthy of the history books. He even wrote three books of the Bible, including Proverbs, Ecclesiastes, and Song of Songs. When his father King David was dying and turning over the kingdom to Solomon, instead of riches and dominance, Solomon prayed that God would give him wisdom. Smooth move, Solomon.

Listen to how God responded, *"Because you have asked for wisdom and not for a long life or wealth or the death of your enemies—I will give you what you asked for! I will give you a wise and understanding heart such as no one else has had or ever will have!* **AND** *I will also give you what you did not ask for—riches and fame! No other king in all the world will be compared to you for the rest of your life!"*

Let that serve as a prayer tip! Let God show up and show off his mighty generosity!

King Solomon wrote about watching men work and sweat under the sun, and one day, he noticed a man working all alone. He had no brothers, sons, friends, or family. Solomon began to ponder and explain the importance of not being alone and developing friendships closer than a brother or a sister.

He tells us that one person alone is easily overpowered, and in previous verses, he shares how one person cannot keep himself warm, his work productivity would be low, and if he fell, he would have no one to help him up. Then Solomon goes on to explain the benefit of having a friend who is there with you side-by-side. The work productivity improves, when you fall, he is there to lift you up, when it's cold, the two could lie bac- to-back to warm up, and if attacked, the two could defend each other.

There is a great story about four friends who had a paralyzed friend. They heard Jesus was going to be in town and knew He could heal their friend. So, they carried their friend on his mat to the house where Jesus was staying. But when they arrived, the house was tiny, and the crowd was huge so they couldn't get to Jesus. In those days, there was no air conditioning, so the roofs were flat and served as a cooler place for people to sleep at night. These four friends climbed up on the roof, carrying their friend on his mat. They literally dug a hole in the roof big enough to lower their friend down into the middle of the crowd right in front of Jesus.

Do you know what Jesus did? The Bible says, "When Jesus saw their faith, He said to the paralytic, 'Son your sins are forgiven—get up and take your mat and walk.'" The paralyzed man was healed because of the faith of his friends! They would not let the kNOTS of paralysis stop them or their friend.

We all need those kinds of friends. More importantly, we need to be faith-filled friends! We need to take the focus off ourselves more and put more focus on modeling the way in such a way that demonstrates our Divine gifts and purpose.

Your Friends, Your Future, and Untying Your kNOTs

In my Make You Matter program, I talk about elevator people. The people who are either taking you up, "elevating you," or those who are dragging and sucking you down. Let me ask you, who are the elevator people in your life? Maybe for this book, we should say they're the people who won't allow you to tie kNOTs or the ones who attempt to secure them around you.

Please spend some time filling out the boxes below.

WHO ARE THE PEOPLE WHO LIFT ME UP?	EXAMPLES OF HOW

WHO ARE THE PEOPLE WHO DRAG ME DOWN?	HOW CAN I LOVE THEM FROM AFAR?

Accepting that some people must be loved from afar is very difficult for most of us. When you make your list, it should become easier to see who's who. Boundaries are necessary for survival, and only YOU can establish and enforce them. Think of it this way: Boundaries aren't to shut other people out; they are to help hold you together.

You may be reading this book, wondering, what if the person who drags me down or tries to kNOT me up is my spouse, my child, a parent, or my boss? For all groups, the very first thing is always prayer. God always hears you, whether you visibly see anything or not.

If any of these relationships are a big Gordian knot, get help! I'm not a counselor, but here is the advice I would give to a friend about people in their life who are dragging them down.

Spouse: I would suggest researching a Christian counselor. Get plugged in with a Christian couple or couple group. Go to a marriage retreat—its a weekend getaway focusing on your marriage. My husband

and I have attended a couple retreats. I love and highly recommend Dr. Gary Chapman's books on love languages. He helps his readers learn how people feel loved in five different ways. Often, we give love the way we want to receive it instead of providing the kind of love that others need from us. It's powerful.

Child: I would ask their age, because knowing if you are still raising them or if they're grown and are sponging off of you would drive my answers. Either way, boundaries must be created. If these are still young children, Dr. Chapman also has a book on love languages for kids.

Parents: I would have similar questions. Being responsible for aging parents is hard, and many need help navigating all that is required. But if it's a case of parents' unwillingness to let you be an adult, those are different answers. In either scenario, there are support groups, and boundaries must be established.

Boss: Not everyone is blessed with a great boss. Fact is, most working people spend more time at work than anywhere else. If you have tried and cannot work it out with your boss, my go-to is, "Life is short!" So my short answer is find another job. It won't be easy, but it will be worth it.

I have found that in most scenarios, things improve with boundaries. Basically, boundaries are establishing what you will and will NOT tolerate. Even in my own marriage, they worked. It was my husband who set the boundaries on ME. He established early in our marriage that he would not tolerate my boss-lady approach to him. It wasn't easy for either of us, but we appear to be living happily ever after now.

As Christians, it is so important to develop relationships with other believers. By having relationships with Christians, we can support, encourage, and stand with one another through all aspects of our lives. Being a Christian in today's society is a difficult challenge, as we are hammered from all sides trying to make us fall, but when we have a Christian support group, we will have the strength to overcome all obstacles and live a life that brings honor and glory to God.

King Solomon wrote "a cord of three strands is not easily broken," describing a potential good knot. This is a wonderful illustration often used in wedding ceremonies when two come together and make God the third strand of their cord. Solomon was referring to the kind of Christian friend, plus God, to form a relationship that is not easily broken.

Both stories help us understand the strength we have when we allow ourselves the blessings of fellow believers being a part of our lives. It's not only them being a part of our lives, but being open with them, sharing our struggles with them as well. By asking for their prayer and support, you can become those three strands of cord that are not easily broken. You can find strength, hope, power, and perseverance as three (you, your friend/spouse, and the Holy Spirit) move forward in overcoming the obstacles you face.

CHAPTER 12

LET *YOUR* LIFE SHINE

*"Today you are you, that is truer than true.
There is no one alive who is youer than you!"*
—Dr. Seuss

Remember the old hymn: *This little light of mine, I'm gonna let it shine... let it shine, let it shine, let it shine?* What does that really mean to let your light shine?

Let's start by talking about light in the most basic form, as we know it. I'm sure where you are there is some type of light. The lights make it easier for you to see. Light exposes and brings clarity. Lights make things brighter.

Thomas Edison, the inventor of the lightbulb, also authored many great quotes, none of which were about light because that was old news to him. He finished that project but used his celebrity status to teach and encourage, which is a perfect example of letting "his light" shine.

Five quick Edison quotes:

- *"I have not failed. I've just found 10,000 ways that won't work."*
- *"Many of life's failures are people who did not realize how close they were to success... when they GAVE UP."*
- *"Our greatest weakness lies in giving up. The most certain way to succeed is always to try just one more time."*
- *"If we did all the things we are capable of, we would literally astound ourselves."*
- *"Genius is 1 percent inspiration and 99 percent perspiration."*

I love the last one because people are often fooled thinking it's the smartest ones who succeed, when in reality, it's typically the ones who dare to WORK HARD! Edison took his real-life experience and celebrity status to shed light and encourage others to:

- Never give up
- Never stop learning
- Never stop trying
- Never stop working hard.

Jesus had a lot to say about light. He said,

- We are the light of the world.
- Our light is not to be hidden, but to stand out and to give light to everyone.
- We are to shine our light so others see or experience our good deeds.
- That through our light, we would glorify God.

I heard a saying once that if you're helping someone and expecting something in return, you are doing business, not kindness.

THE CALL - YOUR LIGHT

When my youngest Taylor was a little girl, I convinced her that President Clinton called me every Saturday to get my advice on the healthcare industry. Obviously, he didn't really call, but she thought it was so cool and often asked me for details about the calls. It was a sad day when I had to come clean with her. I love to watch *The Ellen Show* when she calls people and they lose their minds in excitement!

While it would be awesome to get a call from a famous person, most of us won't ever get that call. But it doesn't matter because there is no worldly call that can compare to the call we all get from God.

I believe in the power of prayer, so that's my first recommendation. Then I would ask yourself a few questions. What do you love or love to do? What are you good at doing? Do other people in your life who you trust talk about what you're good at? If you can answer those three questions with the same answer, BINGO.

When I was young in my career, I held events for physicians and their office staffs. My mom would be in the audience, and I remember one day she told me that the manager of Human Resources told her that I was a really good speaker. I didn't consider myself a speaker (kNOT), but I did LOVE speaking and entertaining the audience. I wished I would have leaned-in to that compliment and pursued my love so much earlier in my career. She might as well have told me the HR manager complimented my shoes. Learn from my mistake and pay attention.

I love to write fun, funny, motivational, and inspiring content. I love to deliver it to audiences. I humbly admit that many people have told me that speaking is my gift. My speaking dream is to give a TED Talk!

We all have a call or gift from God! In fact, it is the most important call we will ever receive because it lays out our future! If we really knew what it meant to be "called by God", kNOTS wouldn't exist in our lives. We wouldn't live, think, or act the way we do now. We would never feel less-than. We would never believe the lies of the devil. We would never allow darkness to loom over us.

DARKNESS:

I like what Martin Luther King Jr. said about darkness. He said, *Darkness cannot drive out darkness; only light can do that. Hate cannot drive out hate; only love can do that.*

I heard a commencement speech a few years ago given by a decorated retired Navy Seal, Admiral William McRaven. He also wrote the book *Make Your Bed*. In his book, he said if you make your bed every morning, that would be your first accomplishment of the day. If you have a cruddy day, when you come home and see the bed, you're reminded of that accomplishment, and it will encourage you. Small but mighty idea!

His commencement speech was a classic change-the-world message, but it was powerful. He talked a lot about the brutal Navy Seal training program. Because of the extreme difficulty, many strong hopeful Seals would "ring the bell," signifying they quit.

One extremely brutal training exercise was the night swim. Before the swim, the trainers debriefed the trainees on all the species of sharks that inhabit the waters. They assured them that no student had ever been eaten by a shark, at least not recently. They were taught that if a shark started circling their position, they were to stand their ground. They were not to swim away and not to show fear, and if the shark, hungry for a midnight snack, should dart toward them, they were to summon up all their strength and punch the shark in the snout, and the shark would turn and swim away.

He used that illustration to remind the graduates that there are a lot of sharks in the world, and if they wanted to complete "their swim," they would have to deal with their sharks. *"If you want to change the world,"* he said, *"don't back down from the sharks."*

One huge job of Navy Seals is conducting underwater attacks against enemy shipping. They practiced it extensively during basic training. The underwater training is where a pair of Seal-divers are dropped off outside an enemy harbor where they then swim over two miles using nothing but a depth gauge and a compass to get to their target.

During that part of the swim, even well below the surface, there is still some light that comes through. He said, *"It was comforting to know there is open water above you."* But as they approach the ship that's tied to a pier, the light begins to fade. Then the steel of the ship blocks all light.

To be successful in the mission, they must swim under the ship and find the keel, which is the center line in the deepest part of the ship. The keel is also the darkest part of the ship where they can't see their hands in front of their faces, where the noise from the ship's machinery is deafening, and where it is so easy to get disoriented and fail.

Every Seal knows that under the keel—at the darkest moment in the mission—is the time they must be calm and composed, when all their tactical skills, all their physical power, and all their inner strength is brought to bear.

And finally, to my point and where he ended his story, which drives home my message. He said, *"If you want to change the world, you must be your very best in the darkest moments."*

Letting Your Light Shine

The Bible says we are to "Shine like the stars in the universe" (Phil. 2:15). How can we shine our light, use our calling for others to see and benefit? What kNOTs are holding us back?

Your light is meant to shine! The brighter your light, the hotter the heat. The higher (brighter) God takes you, the more people will see you! That means the more people you can impact with your light.

How can we shine together? Let's say a thousand people read this book. The average American will meet ten thousand people in their lifetimes—that's a lot! But if every one of us "SHINE OUR LIGHT" and change the lives of just ten people and each of them change the lives of another ten people (only ten!) in five generations, the readers of *Untie Every kNOT* would change the lives of 100 MILLION PEOPLE!

Add one more generation, and that would be ONE BILLION PEOPLE. If you think it's hard to change the lives of ten people, YOU ARE SO WRONG!

 Your light is meant to shine!

One decision to help. One decision to listen without judgment. One decision to make a call to say "I love you," "I miss you," or "I'm thinking about you." One coffee, lunch, dinner, or dessert. One donation. One hug or smile. One choice to not text and drive, not to drink and drive, not to cheat or lie, not to act out in our anger, saying hurtful words that can never be erased. One choice to forgive and love unconditionally.

You all probably know the "you are my sunshine, my only sunshine" song. It is a song that is near and dear to my heart, as it is to many parents who too sang it to their children. I sang it to my daughter well into her adult life. In fact, at her wedding, I used it as my toast to her new husband, saying, *"You are her sunshine, her only sunshine, you make her happy when skies are gray, you'll never know, dear, how much she loves you, please never take her sunshine away."*

HOW BRIGHT IS YOUR LIGHT?

Let me ask you this, if you were arrested tonight for "your bright light," would they have enough evidence to hold you?

HAVE YOU LOST YOUR SPARK?

Do you ever feel like your light just isn't as bright as it used to be or could be? Maybe a situation has dimmed your light. Maybe someone needs to hear this: Your light is not gone! You just need to turn it back on—you control the switch!

STRUGGLES IMPACT SHINE

If there's an event in your life, a trauma or a loss that is trying to block your light or a shadow that is overwhelming you, if it feels like your days have turned to perpetual night, be encouraged! Scripture tells us that night can be as bright as day. Even in the toughest times, we can carry on because there is a light that cannot be extinguished.

The light of God cannot be overcome. His light cannot be put out, and neither can yours! When we are facing God and His light, our back is to the devil. The devil trembles when he hears even God's weakest servant say, *"Yes, Lord, I'll do it!"* Jesus said, "He who follows me will not walk in darkness."

If you find yourself in darkness and want to come into the Light that Jesus provided to everyone, lets pray this simple pray together:

God, I want to come out of the darkness and follow you into a life of light and love. I am a sinner and ask Your forgiveness for all my sins. For all the times I messed up. For all the time I missed out on acknowledging you. Thank you for sending Jesus, your only son, to die for me so that my sins could be washed away, allowing me to spend eternity with YOU. In Jesus' name, AMEN.

If you prayed that prayer, you have just walked out of the darkness!

CHAPTER 13

NOW IS YOUR TIME

At any given moment, you have the power to say, "This is not how my story is going to end."

Dr. Martin Luther King was a legendary giant, man of God, crusader, game-changer, history-maker, and trailblazer! I loved his steadfast bravery combined with such a sense of urgency. He could never be accused of playing it safe. I admire people who step up and step out with their gifts!

In Dr. King's history-making *I Have A Dream* speech, he spoke of the urgency of today, the importance of *NOW!* He was so clear, saying, *"I have a dream TODAY."* He didn't say he had a dream for the future, for next fiscal year, but for now—today!

He said, *"This is no time to engage in the luxury of cooling off or to take the tranquilizing drug of gradualism."* I love that; there is no time to drag our feet.

He was saying that NOW IS THE TIME! He literally said those three words several times in this one speech. He said, *"NOW is the time to make real promises. NOW is the time to rise from the dark and desolate valley. NOW is the time to lift our nation."*

NOW IS THE TIME, NOW IS YOUR TIME

If someone said to you "**NOW IS THE TIME**," how would you respond? Those three words sound pretty urgent. They even have a twinge of danger or intrigue. I guess it would depend on who is saying it, right?

If a stranger on the street or in an airport said "NOW IS THE TIME," with no visible or credible sign of danger or urgency, you would probably ignore them. You would likely physically distance yourself from them, but given the world we live in today, you might investigate the validity a bit.

If a weatherman or weather app showed you proof, i.e., radar that NOW IS THE TIME, you'd probably respond and take cover. Because oftentimes, proof drives action!

I say "oftentimes" because if you've ever been a parent, you know that proof doesn't always drive action. Children often choose to learn the hard way! As "experienced" adults, we scratch our heads and wonder WHY won't they listen to us or trust us.

For the most part, when I sternly told my kids <u>**"NOW!"**</u> they knew any debate was over. While the debate ended, the grunting and eye-rolling certainly did not.

Speaking of family or maybe a friend, if they said NOW is the time, you would probably respond with, *"Now is the time for what?"* Right? You would probably at least give them that courtesy response.

Truth is, the word **NOW** commands attention with a sense of urgency. So, would you agree that your response would almost always be based on the credibility or trust for the person and the evidence or proof that is provided? Yes, of course!

Sadly, too many inspirational and motivational books, words of encouragement, warnings, and *even church messages* become so common that we literally tune them out! Like living on a busy street or highway, you learn to tune it out. Spouses are pros at tuning out! As parents, we become pros as well, especially when it comes to whining.

The truth is, most of us are experts *at tuning "stuff" out*. There is a huge risk because some *things* tuned out can cause us to miss out and subsequently fall out of the blessings God has for each of us.

There's another form of tuning out. It's a form of a kNOT that some may be even more familiar with—it's called disqualification.

You hear about something and are instantly convinced that it does kNOT apply to you. You automatically disqualify yourself, believing you're ineligible for such a time, for such a gift, or for such an opportunity as this. WHY do we do that?

It often doesn't matter if a stranger or a loved one is telling us that NOW is our time. When we've decided to tune out by way of disqualifying ourselves, there will never be our NOW. I want to suggest, perhaps even demonstrate, that **NOW** really is... THE TIME—**YOUR TIME!**

I created a couple of world clouds using words that are synonymous with NOW—words of encouragement, bravery, and hope.

Then, I made a word cloud using words that are antonyms, or opposite of, "NOW." These words are not encouraging but instead incite fear, impossibility, and delay.

It contains words and phrases like: never, later, not now, slowly, after, down the road, in a while, someday, later, eventually, sometime, next, missed the bus, GUS.

Disclaimer: I'm not suggesting anyone be reckless, but too often, you and me, we hide behind the "can kNOT be too reckless" as our excuse. Even if it's not reckless, **NOW** is scary, but God's **plan for you and your life** is never reckless! Scary, maybe. Reckless? NEVER.

The Bible says, *"His blessings make us rich and add **NO** sorrow."* If something seems reckless, look up or get down on your knees as ask, because where God guides, He provides.

What is your favorite day? I hope it is not Someday! You know, the classic, "Someday, I'll do this," or, "Someday, I'll do that." Most of us have a little Someday in us. Start catching yourself using that word, and change that vernacular to a real day.

Teach Us to Number Our Days: Being a NOW Person

We all get the same 1,440 minutes today and every day. What if I told you I could give you that amount in cash every single day? If I promised to have $1,440 on your night stand every morning when you opened your eyes, I bet you would already have plans for that money days, or even longer, in advance. NO WAY would you risk losing that guaranteed money by neglecting to plan for it every day, because just like time, it's use it or lose it!

Unless today is cut short because it's our last, everyone has the same amount of time every day. Why can some people accomplish so much more with the same amount of time?

COMPLACENCY

Who wants this year to be their best year yet or launch their best decade yet? What are you waiting on? What are you putting off doing NOW?

If you wait for perfect conditions, you will never get anything done! Those aren't my words; they came right out of the Bible. It even says **complacency destroys!**

There is a famous Biblical story about a rich man who was going on a long journey and called his three servants together. He told them they would be caretakers of his property while he was gone. The master had carefully assessed the natural abilities of each servant. He gave five talents to one servant, two to another, and one to the third—to each according to his ability. The master then left on his journey.

The person who received the five talents went at once and invested them and made five talents more. As did the one who had the two talents. But the person who had received the one talent went and dug in the ground and hid his master's money.

The talents are really referring to the various gifts and abilities God has given us. It includes our natural abilities and resources—our health, education—as well as our possessions, money, and opportunities. All three acted with a sense of urgency—but not all so wisely.

When the rich man returned, he settled up with each of them. The servant who received the five talents came forward, bringing five talents more, saying, *"Master, you delivered to me five talents; here, I have made five talents more.* The servant who received two talents came forward, saying, *"Master, you delivered to me two talents; here, I have made two talents more.* The master said to both, *"Well done, good and faithful servants. You have been faithful over a little; I will set you over much. Enter into the joy of your master."*

So Far, So Good—But Wait...

The one who received the one talent came forward, saying, *"Master, I knew you to be a hard man. I was afraid and hid the talent in the ground. Here, have what is yours."*

His Master lost his mind, saying, *"You wicked and lazy servant! You should have invested it, and I should have received what was my own with interest.* He took the talent from him and gave it to the servant who had the ten talents, saying, *"For to everyone who has will more be given and he will have an abundance."* He cast the worthless servant into the darkness. Wow, that was a fierce punishment.

The first two guys used the talents and subsequently received more. Then the guy who was responsible for only one talent, when burying it, basically buried himself!

How many of YOU are guilty of hiding or burying your talents? You have to wonder why that guy wasn't motivated. This wasn't a money thing but a lack of desire to serve and fulfill his responsibility in using his talents. He had a lot of excuses too, even trying to blame the master. Let's never fit into that category ever again!

Easy Come, Easy Go!

Just like in that story, opportunities come and opportunities go. What are you waiting for?

Are you waiting to write a book, write a song, go on an adventure, take a trip, teach a class, take a class to advance your career or trade? Are you waiting until the kids are raised, the house is clean, the laundry is done, to get or quit a job? Maybe you're waiting until the weekend, waiting to start on Monday, when the month ends, when the year ends. Maybe you're waiting until you can save money or make more money before you start... Wow, the Bible is right, there are no perfect conditions!

Are you waiting to "get over it," I mean to forgive someone or repair a relationship... but "you're just not ready" because you're just too freaking stubborn? TRUTH: We can't be our best or do our best—NOW or EVER —if we're hanging on to unforgiveness baggage.

Who's waiting to get physically, mentally, or spiritually healthier, by eating right, working out, slowing down, attending church more regularly, but suffers from the battle of the blankets, excuses, or distractions?

Are you waiting because you're a chronic procrastinator? Funny rhyme about procrastination:

Procrastination is my weakness; it only brings me sorrow.
I know I should give it up; in fact, I will tomorrow.

BORN FOR SUCH A TIME AS THIS

There is a true Cinderella story. Her name was Esther,[4] and the events occurred in the capital city of the Persian Empire. Esther's parents died when she was young. She was raised by her cousin Mordecai who held a lower level palace official position. Esther was a beautiful young Jewish woman, and because of some very strange chain of events, she eventually became Queen of a non-Jewish (in fact, an anti-Semitic) country. You can read the whole story in the Book of Esther.

Short version: King Xerxes banished his wife for disobedience. Her disobedience was refusing to come to his drunken guy party and then again refusing to meet with him the next day to talk about it. Banishment was actually a nice sentence. He later regretted it, becoming sad and lonely. His inner circle convinced him to allow them to search the land for all the beautiful virgins from which he could choose. In comes Esther.

It was custom to groom potential Queen candidates, they went through a year of that process. When Esther and the King finally met, he fell in love with her, and they married. Keep in mind, she wasn't his only wife, but apparently, she was highly favored by him. Another twist was that both her religion and relation to Mordecai were kept secret.

In Mordecai's position, years earlier, he intercepted and reported a plot to overthrow and kill King Xerxes, saving his life. That act was recorded but long forgotten. Mordecai **wasn't** part of the King's highest cronies, and he refused to bow to Haman the King's highest official. This infuriated Haman, who wanted to kill him, but instead of laying hands on Mordecai, Haman discovered Mordecai and his people were Jewish and came up a vindictive plot to kill **all the Jews** in the empire, by convincing the King to get rid of "these people" because they don't obey the King's laws.

When Mordecai discovered the plan, he knew their only hope was to get Esther in front of the king to convince him to somehow rescind his order.

She was brave—she didn't come up with excuses, didn't wait to finish up another project, get into better shape, save some getaway money, get a better outfit. NOPE. She heard the calling and took action! She understood NOW was HER time!

Here's the interesting part: Mordecai told her that **even if** she didn't do this, it would happen. God's plan would come to pass, but she would miss the opportunity to be a part of it.

He said, *"If you keep quiet at a time like this, deliverance and relief for the Jews will arise from some other place, but you and your relatives will die* [as a consequence of not taking action]. *Who knows if perhaps you were made queen for just such a time as this?"*

Esther stepped up!

In those days, marriage was much different than it is today. The wife was called up at the pleasure of the king. If she were ever to go uninvited, she could be punished, or worse, sentenced to death. It was a huge risk, so Esther tried to wait to be called, but time was running out and it didn't appear that call would come. So Esther acted, and through a lot of planning and bravery, the tables were turned on Haman, and the Jewish race was saved.

There is much more drama and intrigue to this story. I highly recommend reading it, but to get to the point, I'll skip a few juicy parts.

Imagine if Esther said, "No, I can't, I won't, I'm kNOT capable." If she had allowed herself to get all kNOTTED up in fear that her people would be massacred.

But STOP. Can you imagine if—even though it was God's plan for YOU—you said no to something so unimaginably large? Who knows? What seems small to us can literally be the step sending something so powerful into motion. Ask yourself not "what if," but what will the world miss out on if I don't step up?

That's why I'm telling you what Mordecai told Esther. Who knows if God put you here "FOR SUCH A TIME AS THIS"? God never creates anything without a purpose.

Understand... you have not come this far to only come this far! You were made for so much more! Let me repeat that: You have not come this far to only come this far!

Say it out loud: I HAVE NOT COME THIS FAR TO ONLY COME THIS FAR! Some of you *just* needed those eleven words today! It's not too late, NOT until your heart stops beating.

Did that story ping your heart? What is God waiting for you to do NOW? If you're not going to be a NOW person, who is going to get your gift—your opportunity?

Sadly, who will miss out or potentially suffer or perish because you kept silent and hid your gift?

There are literally opportunities that God brings across our path, your path, my path, that have a limited window, and they're not always going to be there.

I love Robert Frost's poem *Stopping by Woods on a Snowy Evening*. In it, he explains that he cannot linger in the woods to watch the snow fall because he has "promises to keep." Even though the woods capture his attention with their beauty, he makes himself move on to be sure he is true to his word. In a world where promises are often broken, it reminds us to follow through even though we may have miles to go.

> Whose woods these are I think I know.
> His house is in the village though;
> He will not see me stopping here
> To watch his woods fill up with snow.
> My little horse must think it queer
> To stop without a farmhouse near
> Between the woods and frozen lake
> The darkest evening of the year.
>
> He gives his harness bells a shake
> To ask if there is some mistake.
> The only other sound's the sweep
> Of easy wind and downy flake.
> The woods are lovely, dark and deep,
> But I have promises to keep,
> And miles to go before I sleep,
> And miles to go before I sleep.

Don't take the tranquilizing drug of gradualism. Don't disqualify yourself! If you're still alive, so are your gifts and talents. The TIME IS NOW. YOUR TIME IS NOW!

CHAPTER 14

UNTIE YOUR KNOTS TO FINISH GRAND

Ain't life grand?

For years, I've spoken to organizations about going from *Good to Great*, inspired by Jim Collin's book by the same name. While I love the term GREAT, it's just not GREAT enough anymore. I thought, what *is* better than GREAT? What prized memories in my own life—both far in the past and more recent—could perhaps describe something better than GREAT?

As with most things we dedicate time and energy toward, it turns out it wasn't hard at all to come up with an answer. In fact, it was quick and obvious. My mind kept landing on memories of my full-of-life, crazy-happy grandmother.

Life was grand when she was near. Her cooking was grand. Her attitude was grand. Her capacity to love was grand. Her storytelling was grand; so grand, in fact, we weren't always sure it was 100 percent accurate. Today, if someone in my family "embellishes" a story, we fondly respond with an *"OKAY, Grandma!"* Learning how to live grand came from every single memory of my grandmother.

Now I get to watch my own wonderful parents keep the grandparenting traditions alive with my children. Most importantly as grandparents, my parents remind me through their actions not to judge children by adult standards but to show them grace and let them be children, remembering that we can learn as much from them as they learn from us.

So there it was, bigger and better than great: It's **GRAND!** I was blessed to have had the most incredible example of being GRAND. And with that as my measuring stick, I applied GRAND to key areas where we all can perhaps make a big impact and ultimately leave a GRAND legacy.

START GRAND. Did you know the Bible says we all have angels assigned to us? Now that's GRAND! The sad news is that most of our angels are so bored because we don't give them the authority to act. We can either handcuff them or authorize their abilities to guide us and protect us, and that starts the minute we open our eyes. Don't hit that snooze button. Pop right up and welcome the day. We're alive another day—isn't that enough to start the grand process? When our feet hit the floor each morning, we want our angels going right to work and the devil to scream, "Oh crap, he or she is up!" That's starting grand!

What gets us frazzled and off to a not-so-grand start? Often, with a little adjustment the night before, we could completely transform a crazy start into a grand start. Waiting until the morning to pick out what we're going to wear or decide what to pack for lunches can create a snowball of stress first thing in the morning. To help start our days grand, it might be helpful to spend a few minutes the night before planning and even reading something positive before going to sleep. That puts a nice end to each day and ultimately leads to welcoming in the grand new day.

THINK GRAND. We are what we think about! That's scary! Every action starts with a thought—good or bad. Sometimes, completely out of nowhere, a negative thought pops into our minds. Just because it pops into our heads doesn't mean we have to own it! If a spider landed on us, we would swat it off (or kill it) immediately! Think of a bad thought the same way. We all experience unsolicited and unwanted negative thoughts, sometimes more often than we want to admit. Just don't let them stick around! As quickly as a bad thought pops into our heads, we must think to ourselves, "That is **NOT** my thought!" Don't be a percolator of negative thoughts that brew and grow into negative speech and then negative actions! Make it a habit to find something good about everyone. When I'm struggling to find something good to think about someone, I ask God to help me see that person the way He sees them. It works every time!

SPEAK GRAND. Everything we say impacts our life in one way or another. Remember those angels? Here's where it starts, by speaking GRAND. We don't want to handcuff our angels by speaking negatively. For example, when the alarm goes off, don't hit it and say, "I hate getting up so early," or "I'm exhausted," or "I hate my job" because when we speak negatively, we create a negative impact. Instead, speak life, speak prosperity—whatever it is, speak positively. Speak things like, "Today is going to be a grand day!" or, "I got another day to do something grand!"

I looked for every version in scripture that starts with "He said" or "the Lord Said." Why? Because if God said it, you can always count on it! I wrote down a few that I speak out loud daily. A few examples include:

- You said that You gave me the spirit of power, love, & self-discipline. *(And oh, how I need that self-discipline to step away from those Girl Scout cookies!)*
- You said You would fight for me. *(No fighting for me today, you'll do it for me.)*
- You said overwhelming victory is mine through Christ. *(Wow, not just victory, but overwhelming victory? BRING IT ON!)*
- You said I am not normal, so don't act it—rise above and set the example.
- You said Your plan for me is for good and not disaster, for a future and hope.
- You said You will rescue me. *(So I think I'll take some risks today and write this blog.)*
- You said You're in control of all my situations *(even though I'm a control freak).*

- You said You order Your angels to protect us where we go.
- You said I should be persistent whether the time is favorable or not.
- You said You made me as hard as a rock, so don't be afraid or fear ugly looks. *(I will not fear anyone who rolls their eyes.)*
- You said, say this is what the Sovereign Lord says whether they listen or not.

If we continue to speak GRAND, soon, instead of saying "God, You said," we'll be saying, "God, You DID!"

Since I was blessed *(some may think cursed)* with an outspoken personality, my mouth is something I must work on daily. When I read Malachi 3:16, which says, "God records our conversations," that got my attention! I put that on a Post-it note above my computer monitor to remind me that His holy recorder is on me... a holy reminder to "ZIP IT, SKIPPY!"

ACT GRAND even when no one is watching. Our actions speak *so loudly* that people won't hear what we're saying! Whether we believe it or not, actions really DO speak louder than words. We have no idea how many times *every day* our actions (good or bad) impact others. Like the way we act when we're asked to wait in line. The way we act over the telephone when we can't be seen.

We should always act in such a way that people who witness our actions, our acts of kindness, consideration, and respect, want to *be* better, *do* better, and *act* better because of what they've witnessed us doing. Frequently, teachers say, *"The apple doesn't fall far from the tree."* Good or bad, how we act is how our children will act. Our actions gave them permission. Small ears and eyes are often close by!

I always hear my mom say, "You are who you hang with." Spend time with people you want to act like. Hang out with people as long as you're affecting them and they're not infecting you.

FORGIVE GRAND. Holding onto unforgiveness is like drinking poison and expecting someone else to get sick. Nothing in this world bears the imprint of the Son of God so surely as forgiveness. Release yourself by forgiving grandly.

SHINE GRAND. Do you know of a person who is so full of life they light up a room? They're the same people that when they leave the room, it feels like the oxygen just left as well. Who wouldn't want to shine that grand?

CELEBRATE GRAND. We live in a free country, and since most of us have never known anything else, it is very easy to forget the immeasurable value of our freedom by taking it for granted—about a thousand times each day. We get to read what we want, watch what we want, say what we want, buy what we want, vote for whom we want, eat what we want, and above all, have the freedom to worship whom we want. Shall I go on? Every single day, we have something grand to celebrate!

STAND GRAND, which is the opposite of grand stand! By this I mean, "Take a stand." Silence is interpreted as approval. When we hear, or worse, participate, in gossip, we are fully in agreement unless we lovingly speak out for what is right. It's easier said than done sometimes, but worse is the regret of not standing GRAND for what is right!

SERVE GRAND. I don't know about you, but every time I serve in any capacity without expecting anything in return, I feel completely energized. There is nothing like serving others. This is an area I need to work on because I selfishly think that as long as my plate is full and I genuinely don't have extra time, it is okay not to reach out to serve others. That couldn't be further from the truth. To serve is a grand act of selflessness.

PRAY GRAND. If we are praying, something is happening in the lives of those for whom we pray, whether we see it or not. We stand the strongest and tallest on our knees. On our knees, we can get God's vision. Remember ,God said His plan for us is to prosper and not harm, to give hope and a future. There are more than 7,000 promises buried in the Bible, most of which are targeted for me and you. When we pray, we stop looking at our problems and instead look at our problem solver. There is no grander place than in prayer.

FINISH GRAND. It's **kNOT** how we start the race; it's how we finish it. But we must stay in the race! If we quit, we lose. The way to be encouraged is to encourage others. There have been so many stories in history about people who have quit because they just couldn't *see* the finish line. Don't be blinded by adversity or difficulties. Don't be afraid to ask for help. Remember, when God calls us, He gives us all we need to accomplish it. Feeling inadequate is not uncommon—it shows we need God. When it feels the hardest is often when we're the closest to the finish! Pace yourself, stay the course, and ***finish grand.***

THE kNOT Prayer

Unknown author

Please untie the kNOTS that are in my mind and in my life.

Remove the have-kNOTS, the can-kNOTS,
and the do-kNOTS that I have in my mind.

Erase the will-kNOTS, may-kNOTS,
might-kNOTS that may find a home in my heart.

Release me from the could-kNOTS, would-kNOTS, and

should-kNOTS that obstruct my life.

And most of all, I ask that you remove from my mind,
my heart, and my life

all the am kNOTS that I have allowed to hold me back,

especially the thought that I am kNOT good enough.

AMEN!

Conclusion

 It's not what you know—it's what you do with what you know that matters.

With the demands of our fast-paced lives and culture, it's so hard to invest quality time in ourselves. YOU DID IT! I'm sure it wasn't easy. You're awesome! Now what?

While reading this book, how many times did you recognize yourself or someone you love? I bet a lot—because until we're aware of the debilitating effects of kNOTS, they're hard to recognize. Moreover, it's a hard pill to swallow knowing we are responsible for tying most of them. The good news is, if we tie them, we can certainly untie them.

My prayer is that you realize your ability to recognize a kNOT forming before it's able to take root. My friend, you are fully equipped and capable to Untie Every kNOT.

Be blessed.

Review Inquiry

Hey, it's Tammy here.

I hope you've enjoyed the book, finding it both useful and fun. I have a favor to ask you.

Would you consider giving it a rating wherever you bought the book? Online book stores are more likely to promote a book when they feel good about its content, and reader reviews are a great barometer for a book's quality.

So please go to the website of wherever you bought the book, search for my name and the book title, and leave a review. If able, perhaps consider adding a picture of you holding the book. That increases the likelihood your review will be accepted!

Many thanks in advance,

Tammy Tiller-Hewitt

Will You Share the Love?

***Get this book for a friend,
associate, or family member!***

If you have found this book valuable and know others who would find it useful, consider buying them a copy as a gift. Special bulk discounts are available if you would like your whole team or organization to benefit from reading this.

Just contact tth@tillerhewitt.com
or visit
Untieeveryknot.com or
TammyTillerHewitt.com.

Would You Like Tammy to Speak to Your Organization?

BOOK TAMMY NOW!

To have Tammy speak to your organization about the principles found in *Untie Every kNOT* or other success insights, email speaker@UntieEverykNOT.com.

Here's what audiences are saying, from Mayo Clinic to leadership and corporate conferences:

- "Tammy's energy level is infectious, time flew by."
- "I love Tammy! I could listen to her all day. She is phenomenal."
- "So needed! Absolutely love that this type of content was added for the conference."
- "Tammy is a great presenter and love listening to her."
- "Tammy is a dynamic speaker. There were points that she shared in this presentation that I know I'll be thinking about for a long time."
- "Filled with high energy and practical ideas."
- "It was great. Well worth my time!"

- "Such a fantastic program! Tammy's approach is now my 'go-to!'"
- "Tammy really inspired me and gave me some creative ideas about overcoming objections."
- "Tammy has great enthusiasm and presentation skills!"
- "Interesting stats, great relevant examples and exercises."
- "Information was presented in an upbeat and fun manner!"
- "Tammy is awesome and the message is clear, concise, and completely on target."

To learn how you can bring her message to
your organization, email **tth@tillerhewitt.com** or visit
Untieeveryknot.com or **TammyTillerHewitt.com**.

ENDNOTES

1. 1 Corinthians 14:33

2. Proverbs 4:23

3. The Chicken and an Eagle "Choices & Illusions" By Elden Taylor

4. The book of Esther, Holy Bible

ABOUT THE AUTHOR

Tammy Tiller-Hewitt is a nationally recognized speaker, leadership advisor and author. Tammy's day job is working nationally with healthcare organizations and leaders, while simultaneously living her dream job of leading millions to discover their "WHY," or purpose. Through her dream work, she has found most people struggle in discovering their purpose only because of their own self-imposed kNOTS. *That led her to write Untie Every kNOT: Discover What kNOTS Are Causing You to Miss Out, Chicken Out, or Be Counted Out!*

Tammy serves as President & Chief Motivational Officer for one of the nation's leading healthcare consulting firms specializing in strategic growth and physician engagement. She is well-versed in helping organizations and their leaders untie corporate-sized kNOTS so they can achieve abundant growth. She earned an undergraduate degree in Marketing, a master's degree in Healthcare Administration, and is a Fellow of the American College of Healthcare Executives. She is also a certified leadership coach, trainer, and speaker.

Tammy is also a proud member of the teaching team at Enjoy Church, a large non-denominational Christian church in the greater St. Louis, Missouri, area.

Tammy is a woman of faith, a wife, mother, mimi, daughter, sister, friend, and avid connoisseur of all things sweet! If you want to book a fun, funny, and motivational speaker, BOOK TAMMY TO SPEAK.

EMAIL: tth@tillerhewitt.com

WEBSITE: Untieeveryknot.com or TammyTillerHewitt.com

Made in the USA
Monee, IL
19 November 2020